SpringerBriefs in Computer Science

SpringerBriefs present concise summaries of cutting-edge research and practical applications across a wide spectrum of fields. Featuring compact volumes of 50 to 125 pages, the series covers a range of content from professional to academic.

Typical topics might include:

- A timely report of state-of-the art analytical techniques
- A bridge between new research results, as published in journal articles, and a contextual literature review
- A snapshot of a hot or emerging topic
- An in-depth case study or clinical example
- A presentation of core concepts that students must understand in order to make independent contributions

Briefs allow authors to present their ideas and readers to absorb them with minimal time investment. Briefs will be published as part of Springer's eBook collection, with millions of users worldwide. In addition, Briefs will be available for individual print and electronic purchase. Briefs are characterized by fast, global electronic dissemination, standard publishing contracts, easy-to-use manuscript preparation and formatting guidelines, and expedited production schedules. We aim for publication 8–12 weeks after acceptance. Both solicited and unsolicited manuscripts are considered for publication in this series.

**Indexing: This series is indexed in Scopus, Ei-Compendex, and zbMATH **

Thor Myklebust • Tor Stålhane •
Dorthea Mathilde Kristin Vatn

The AI Act and
The Agile Safety Plan

Springer

Thor Myklebust
Software Engineering, Safety and Security
SINTEF Digital
Trondheim, Norway

Tor Stålhane
Department of Computer Science
NTNU
Gjøvik, Norway

Dorthea Mathilde Kristin Vatn
SINTEF
Trondheim, Norway

ISSN 2191-5768   ISSN 2191-5776   (electronic)
SpringerBriefs in Computer Science
ISBN 978-3-031-80503-5   ISBN 978-3-031-80504-2   (eBook)
https://doi.org/10.1007/978-3-031-80504-2

This work was supported by NTNU and SINTEF.

This Springer imprint is published by the registered company Springer Nature Switzerland AG
The registered company address is: Gewerbestrasse 11, 6330 Cham, Switzerland

If disposing of this product, please recycle the paper.

Preface

The EU AI Act will have major implications on the development, implementation, and use of high risk systems. This book builds on the tradition of establishing safety plans in the development of high risk systems. It also addresses how the AI Act, as a new comprehensive legal framework, will affect the content of a safety plan.

The content of the safety plan has direct implications for the final safety case that is a prerequisite before the system is placed on the market. The purpose of this book is therefore to support developers of high risk systems establishing an efficient safety plan in the development phase while ensuring that the final product is compliant with relevant standards and regulations. Therefore, the main contribution of this book is threefold:

1. Provide an overview over all the different topics and issues that should be addressed in a safety plan when developing high risk systems
2. Explain how the EU AI Act and other relevant standards and regulations are relevant to achieve compliance in the context of high risk system development
3. Provide a clear link between the safety plan and the content of the safety cases, ensuring that safety cases efficiently can be established when the final product(s) is sent to the market

The main features of this book are as follows:

- It is a reference book building on established standards
- It facilitates development projects, ensuring that compliance aspects are considered at an early point
- It covers new topics such as human oversight and organizational aspects
- It should facilitate the development of the safety case
- It should ensure that changes and developments in both technology and regulation can be handled efficiently

- It improves the overall safety work, ensuring that it has structure and direction.
- It includes relevant agile topics across all the chapters.

Trondheim, Norway   Thor Myklebust
Gjøvik, Norway   Tor Stålhane
Trondheim, Norway   Dorthea Mathilde Kristin Vatn

Acknowledgement

We would like to thank the Research Council of Norway for co-funding the work leading to this book as part of two projects:

- "TrustMe", project no.: 309207
- "Integrated Service & Safety Platform", project number: 309406

Gratitude is extended to NTNU and SINTEF Digital for facilitating the necessary funding, which enabled the publication of this book as an open-access resource.

The following experts generously contributed their time and expertise to review this book, leading to significant enhancements in its quality:

- Christoph Thieme, Researcher at SINTEF Digital
- Maria V. Ottermo, Research Manager at SINTEF Digital

The authors also thank EASA and Daedalean (2024), as well as Hawkins et al. (2022), for permission to reproduce figures.

Last but not least, we are grateful for Springer's layout and editorial comments and for their effective and professional work.

Contents

Appendices

Chapter 1
Introduction to the Book

Artificial Intelligence (AI) systems have become a major part of many industries and will most likely become increasingly complex, used for more applications, also within the safety-critical domain. This book aims to provide the reader with some basic insight into the AI Act (REGULATION (EU) 2024/1689) and its relevance for the development of high risk systems. The main part of the book is developed to cover all relevant topics in a safety plan, which should serve as a foundation for developing future safety cases for AI safety systems. The book should be relevant for experts and stakeholders involved in developing high risk systems, both manufacturers and operators. The book is also relevant for those having an interest in how the AI Act impacts technology development processes generally. As such, especially start-ups and small and medium-sized enterprises will find this book useful.

High risk AI systems, which are the focus of this book, are subject to stringent requirements. Our focus is on generic functional safety (FuSa) in line with IEC 61508, but domain-specific automotive, railway, and, to some degree, seaborne systems are also addressed. We seek to cover a broad set of relevant topics to be considered when developing a safety plan in product development projects. We aim to cover both aspects relevant to development projects of safety-critical technologies generally and aspects that could be considered specifically relevant to the development of high risk AI systems. In addition to covering aspects relating to the technical dimensions, we also cover human and organizational aspects, emphasizing the importance of stakeholder considerations and inclusion when developing high risk AI systems.

To serve as an introduction to this book, we will first provide the reader with insights into some major topics that are relevant for the comprehension of the rest of the book. This chapter therefore consists of five sections we believe are essential to have as a background. Section 1.1 focuses on how the AI Act defines AI and how it categorizes AI systems into four risk levels. In relation to this, we also discuss how the AI Act places obligations on the stakeholders involved in the high risk AI supply chain and provide a brief note on market access and how the AI Act relates to the New Legislative Framework adopted by the EU in 2008. Section 1.2 provides

© The Author(s) 2025
T. Myklebust et al., *The AI Act and The Agile Safety Plan*, SpringerBriefs in Computer Science, https://doi.org/10.1007/978-3-031-80504-2_1

some basic insights into standards organizations and the standardization process. Knowledge of these processes is important to efficiently operate in the complex compliance landscape of high risk AI systems, facilitating the establishment of cost-effective design solutions and trustworthy safety cases. Section 1.3 provides some basic insights into the agile approach that has been guiding our work with the agile safety plan (Myklebust et al., 2016a), as we believe having an agile approach facilitates that both existing and coming requirements can be satisfied more efficiently. Section 1.4 gives a brief note on how the agile safety plan relates to the final safety case that should be developed for the high risk system. Section 1.5 gives an overview of the structure of each chapter in this book, hopefully making it easier to navigate the book and use it as a reference tool.

1.1   EU AI Act

The EU AI Act, a comprehensive legal framework, is designed to ensure the safe, secure, and trustworthy development and deployment of AI systems across the European Union (EU) and the European Economic Area (EEA). By providing regulations and guidelines, the Act fosters a strong emphasis on the protection of fundamental rights, reassuring the audience about the ethical considerations in AI development.

The EU AI Act defines AI broadly, stating that an AI system *"means a machine-based system that is designed to operate with varying levels of autonomy and that may exhibit adaptiveness after deployment, and that, for explicit or implicit objectives, infers, from the input it receives, how to generate outputs such as predictions, content, recommendations, or decisions that can influence physical or virtual environments"* (AI Act Article 3, p. 46). The broad definition above encompasses rule-based systems, machine learning, and neural networks. The definition ensures that a wide range of AI technologies are covered under the regulation. The EU AI Act's risk-based approach (Article 9) is an important aspect of the Act's regulation of AI. This approach underscores the Act's commitment to prioritizing safety and protecting the fundamental rights of individuals in developing and deploying AI systems. It categorizes AI systems into four distinct risk levels: unacceptable, high, limited, and minimal. The high risk AI systems that are the focus of this book are subject to stringent requirements. This category includes AI applications in critical infrastructure, education, employment, essential services, law enforcement, and migration. High risk AI systems can significantly impact health, safety, and fundamental human rights. Examples include AI systems used in medical devices, autonomous vehicles, and critical infrastructure management. To be made available on the market, these systems must undergo rigorous assessments and adhere to strict documentation and transparency requirements.

The EU AI Act (Article 2 "Scope" and Article 40 "Harmonised standards and standardisation deliverables") has a scope encompassing all stakeholders involved in the AI ecosystem, including providers, deployers, importers, distributors, product manufacturers, and authorized representatives. The Act aims to regulate the entire lifecycle of AI systems, from development to deployment and post-market monitoring. The EU AI Act places obligations on all stakeholders involved in the high risk AI supply chain. Providers of AI systems, such as developers and manufacturers, must ensure compliance with regulatory requirements, including transparency, safety, and robustness. Entities using AI systems must adhere to safe deployment and standards and include effective monitoring and human oversight. Importers and distributors must ensure that AI systems entering the EU market comply with the Act's standards. Product manufacturers and authorized representatives are responsible for maintaining detailed technical documentation and ensuring conformity with the Act's provisions.

Regarding Market Access and Standards, the EU AI Act promotes the use of harmonized standards (HS) and conformity assessments to ensure a harmonized approach to AI regulation. Notified bodies (section IV of the EU AI Act) will play a crucial role in assessing the compliance of high risk AI systems. Additionally, the Act encourages the development and use of common standards to facilitate market access and ensure consistency across the EU.

EU Legislative Framework and Link to the AI Act
Having insights into the existing EU legislative framework is also key when understanding the implications of the AI Act on high risk systems. The EU adopted the New Legislative Framework (NLF) already in 2008 with the aim of improving the internal market for goods and to strengthen the conditions for placing a wide range of products on the EU market. This NLF includes several of the important aspects that are included in the AI Act that are relevant for high risk systems and the agile safety plan. The topics related to an agile safety plan are, e.g., harmonized standards (AI Act Article 40), declaration of conformity (AI Act Article 47), and CE marking (AI Act Article 48). The Blue Guide (EA, 2022) is a comprehensive resource that provides a deep understanding of the NLF. It covers important elements such as accreditation (AI Act Articles 28, 29, and 30), product marketing (AI Act Article 31), and market surveillance (mentioned 175 times in the AI Act), empowering you to navigate the intricacies of the NLF with confidence.

1.2   Standards

Organizations like ISO, IEEE, and IEC play a crucial part in developing AI systems, and they handle the creation of documents in similar ways. Current risk assessment methods in domains like railway, automotive, and seaborne are not fully applicable to AI, which presents new, unique, difficult, and complex risks. The standardization process involves several key documents, each serving a purpose and developed at different stages. These documents include the Public Available Specification (PAS), Technical Specification (TS), Technical Report (TR), and the International Standards (IS), as shown in the figure below. The differences between these documents are primarily related to the approval processes, the maturity of the technology the standards are developed for, and whether the guidelines should be considered informative or normative. It is crucial to understand these documents in order to navigate the standardization process effectively. International standard organizations' response to rapid technology development is often an agile/lean approach. Having the possibility to start with a TR, then improve it to a TS or PAS, and then later issue an international standard (IS) can be considered a Minimum Viable Product (MVP) approach for international standard organizations, enabling an accessible document early on with enough content to be useful for both manufacturers and authorities.

The EU has a goal to develop harmonized standards (HS) for topics that are relevant to high risk AI systems. EU [Link1 to EU] provides the following definition of a harmonized standard: *"A harmonized standard is a European standard developed by a recognized European Standards Organisation: CEN, CENELEC, or ETSI. Manufacturers, other economic operators, or conformity assessment bodies can use harmonised standards to demonstrate that products, services, or processes comply with relevant EU legislation. The references of harmonised standards must be published in the Official Journal of the European Union (OJEU)."* Before a standard becomes harmonized it must include both the essential and other relevant legal requirements that will be covered by the standard, in what is commonly named "Annex ZZ". In addition, the standard has to be listed in the OJEU.

The next edition of functional safety standards, e.g. IEC 61508, will refer to existing and future standards like ISO/IEC TR 5469:2024 for Functional Safety and AI systems, which will evolve in the near future. ISO/IEC TR 5469:2024 is already being improved and will be issued as ISO/IEC TS 22440 in 2025 or 2026. This TS will be issued in three parts: 1 Requirements, 2 Guidance, and 3 Examples of application. Later, we expect that ISO/IEC TS 22440 will be improved and extended with an Annex ZZ (Fig. 1.1) to become a harmonized standard. The annex will be like a checklist that helps practitioners who follow the standard to also follow the law.

As the "Annex ZZ" part is a key characteristic of a harmonized standard, we exemplify what this might look like with a copy from Annex ZZ of EN 50126–1:2017 (Railway) *"This European Standard has been prepared under a mandate given to CENELEC by the European Commission and the European Free Trade Association and within its scope the standard covers all relevant essential requirements as given in Annex Ill of the EC Directive 2008/57/EC (also named as New Approach Directive 2008/57/EC Rail Systems: Interoperability). Once this standard is cited in the Official Journal of the European Union under that Directive and has been*

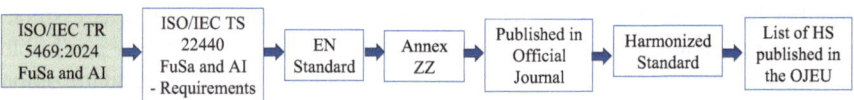

Fig. 1.1 From TR to harmonized standards listed in the OJEU

implemented as a national standard in at least one Member State, compliance with the clauses of this standard given in Table ZZ.1 for "Control-Command and Signalling", Table ZZ.2 "Locomotives and Passenger Rolling Stock", Table ZZ.3 for "Energy", Table ZZ.4 for "Infrastructure" confers, within the limits of the scope of this standard, a presumption of conformity with the corresponding Essential Requirements of that Directive and associated EFTA regulations".

In addition to generic Functional Safety and AI standards, other domain-specific standards, like ISO/PAS 8800: 2024-12 Road Vehicles—Safety has recently been issued. For further information regarding harmonized standards, see Chapter 8 of this book.

1.3   How the Safety Plan Relates to the Safety Case

While our book outlines all the relevant aspects one should consider when developing a safety plan, it is worth emphasizing early on how the work with the safety plan has a direct impact on and relevance for *safety case* development.

The development and use of safety cases have a long tradition within railways, and the much-used railway standard EN 50129:18 divides the safety case into six parts: Definition of System, Quality Management Report, Safety Management Report, Technical Safety Report, Related Safety Cases, and Conclusion. While this is a structure that sufficiently has covered relevant aspects in a railway context, we believe that future safety case approaches aiming to cover new domains, such as the automotive, the maritime, or the nuclear domain, should include new parts. This need is also made more relevant with the increasing introduction of AI into these domains. We therefore suggest that future safety cases should include four additional parts: Operational Design Domain (ODD), Concept of Operation (ConOps), AI Safety Report (ASR), and Human Aspects and Oversight (HAO) (Myklebust et al., 2025). We believe that adding these new parts provides a solid foundation for future safety case development while ensuring that our safety plan is more relevant to a broader audience. Also, we believe that incorporating these topics can foster collaboration among multidisciplinary teams, allowing each group to focus on their specific areas of expertise and responsibility, all the while contributing to the overall success of the safety plan.

Table 1.1 provides an overview of all the different safety case parts, and we illustrate how the different parts of the safety case can be built on the different safety plan chapters in this book. We believe that a clear understanding of how the safety plan relates to the final safety case facilitates an efficient process of establishing the safety case, hindering that parts of the process are done twice. While Chap. 18 presents further information on safety case development, we believe that providing a foreshadowing of the link between the safety plan and the safety case in the introduction serves as a useful basis for the reader.

Table 1.1 Link between safety case chapters and the safety plan chapters in this book

Safety case parts	Description	Safety plan chapters
0: Introduction	Presents the purpose, scope, and specified safety lifecycle phases while outlining the policy and limitations	2, 8, 11
1: Definition of System (DoS)	Define and provide references to the system, subsystems, products, or equipment to which the safety case shall refer, including version numbers and modification status of all requirements	3
2: Operational Design Domain (ODD)	Presents the operating environment within which a safety system can safely perform its operations	3
3: Concept of Operation (ConOps)	Presents the users, system's operational scenarios, and intended purpose	3
4: Quality Management Report (QMR)	Details the quality processes and measures implemented to ensure that the system meets the required quality standards throughout development	5, 7, 13, 15, 19
5: Safety Management Report (SMR)	Documents the safety activities performed to ensure effective safety management throughout the project lifecycles	4, 8, 9, 10, 11, 12, 13, 14, 18
6: Technical Safety Report (TSR)	Provides detailed information regarding the system's technical safety aspects, excluding AI-related data and SW	4, 5
7: AI Safety Report (ASR)	Present evidence for the safe integration of AI technologies within safety-related systems	5, 6, 10, 17
8: Human aspects and oversight (HAO)	Presents issues related to human factors, i.e. design of human-machine interfaces, situational awareness, and controllability	16
9: Related safety cases (RSC)	Presents the system's RSCs, which include subsystems, products, modules, items, or equipment on which the system under consideration depends	18.2
10: Conclusion	Summarizes the evidence and main arguments from the safety case, confirming that the system is adequately safe and complies with relevant standards	Na

1.4   AI Safety and Agile Development

While developers of high risk systems traditionally followed and many still follow a waterfall/V development process, this book is based on an agile approach. We believe that an agile approach facilitates more efficient compliance with both existing and upcoming regulations. Also, as most products will be updated and developed through DevOps after being put into use, an agile approach will be necessary.

To ensure that all requirements in the EU AI Act and relevant safety standards can be satisfied, we have analysed the AI Act, the AI standard ISO/IEC 5338:2023, and safety standards such as EN 50128:2011, EN 50716:2023, IEC 61508-3:2010, and the ISO 26262-6:2018 software safety standards. The acquired information in combination with an agile safety approach such as SafeScrum (Hanssen et al., 2018) serves as a basis for developing the agile safety plan (Myklebust et al., 2016a) that satisfies the requirements of these standards while enabling an agile development process.

The purpose of the agile safety plan can be summarized as an attempt to aid manufacturers and other stakeholders mentioned in the AI Act in achieving certification or internal approval of their products by satisfying its requirements. The agile safety plan is to be used together with other relevant plans (see Annex A of this book). Table 1.2 lists relevant agile practices that may be used when developing high risk AI systems. A *practice* in software (SW) development is a working, repeatable activity. Most practices in Table 1.2 have been used in our safety-related projects. Some have been adapted by the authors (Myklebust et al., 2018a), while others have been developed by the authors of this book (Myklebust et al., 2019). By presenting various practices, teams can select those most suited to their project needs and context, enhancing productivity and communications. Normally, we evaluate which practices shall be used early in the project.

Table 1.2 Agile practices that have been used in one or more of our projects

1. A/B testing	18. Daily scrum	36. Open office space	55. Sprint planning
2. Acceptance testing	19. Definition of done	37. Onsite customer	56. Sprint retrospective
3. AFD, Analyse first development	20. Definition of ready	38. Prioritized work list Product owner	57. Sprint review
4. Agile UX (user experience)	21. Epic	39. Product road mapping	58. Stepwise integration story
5. Automated build	22. Fail first	40. Pull	59. Task board
6. Automated tests	23. First principle (what is it made of)	41. Quick design session	60. Team-based estimation
7. Burn down chart	24. 40 h week	42. Rapid prototyping	61. Team communication
8. Backlog (books)	25. Frequent releases	43. Refactoring	62. Test-driven requirement
9. Backlog refinement	26. Hazard story	44. Release plan	63. Test first devlopment
10. Backlog splitting	27. Incremental	45. Relative estimation	64. The wall
11. Backlog (product backlog)	28. Information radiators	46. Safety story	65. Time box
12. BDD (behaviour-driven development)	29. Integration	47. Security story	66. Unit testing
13. Canary testing	30. Iteration	48. Simple design	67. Usability testing
14. Coding standard	31. MCP, Minimum Certifiable Product	49. Shippable code	68. User story (vertical user story)
15. Common work area	32. Model storming	50. Shippable documents	69. Velocity
16. Collective code ownership	33. MVP (Minimum Viable Product)	51. Shippable HW	70. Vertical slice
17. Continuous deployment	34. MVS (Minimum Viable System)	52. Short iterations	
	35. MVP-SC (MVP-safety case)	53. Spike	
		54. Sprint (SafeScrum and FuSa sprint)	

1.5   Structure of the Agile Safety Plan

Each chapter includes objectives, references to the safety case and relevant documents, and details on processes, practices, and challenging issues to provide a comprehensive safety framework. Below we have described in more detail the structure for each chapter in the agile safety plan part of this book.

Objective
In each chapter, we have included objectives for the chapter of the agile safety plan to provide a clear overview of the relevant challenges the chapter aims to address. This approach helps both experts and non-experts to understand the purpose and focus of the chapter, making it easier to grasp and navigate the safety requirements.

Information
This section will provide relevant links to safety case parts (see 1.3 above) and relevant documents that should be referenced in relation to that topic. In this way, we aim to facilitate a link between the safety plan and the safety case, which should be considered the final goal. Relevant software documents are listed in the Annex A of this book.

Requirements
This part includes requirements related to the AI Act (Regulation 2024/1689), AI and safety standards such as ISO/IEC 5469, IEC 61508 series, and ISO 26262 series, and other regulations and directives in some chapters.

Agile Adaptation (When Relevant)
This part of the chapter includes relevant topics, iterative and incremental development, and relevant processes and practices.

Safety Plan Issues
Challenging issues related to the safety plan are mentioned and commented.

References
References are provided at the end of the book. We have divided the references in three lists: (1) References to EU regulations and directives, (2) References to standards, and (3) References to literature and other sources.

Chapter 2
The Agile Safety Plan

This chapter introduces the agile safety plan concept and gives a brief overview of its history. Next, it defines some key terms related to developing and implementing strategies for achieving functional safety. Lastly, it provides a brief note on the purpose, scope, and context of the safety plan and notes the importance of communicating the system's limitations and assumptions.

2.1 Introduction to the Agile Safety Plan

Safety plans have been long required for certifying and approving safety-critical systems. Developing a safety plan is an efficient method for helping the developers of high risk AI systems to focus on the simple but important question:

How do you ensure that you develop a safe system?

The main goal of the safety plan is to develop one or more safety cases and ensure that the product or system can be certified and, when necessary, approved by relevant authorities.

This book covers all the relevant chapters of the safety plan. Its structure allows for breaking the safety plan into smaller components, facilitating flexibility and adaptability. This might be considered especially useful because organizations must effectively respond to new information and rapid technology development without disrupting their overall safety strategy. Our agile safety plan was initially developed in 2015 and presented in a paper in 2016 (Myklebust et al., 2016a). The agile safety

© The Author(s) 2025
T. Myklebust et al., *The AI Act and The Agile Safety Plan*, SpringerBriefs in Computer Science, https://doi.org/10.1007/978-3-031-80504-2_2

plan was further developed as part of real-world development projects for the railway and process industry domains. The improvements were published in *The Agile Safety Case* in 2018 (Myklebust & Stålhane, 2018). Later, we have suggested that the traditional safety case parts in EN 50129 for the railway should be extended with several parts due to the increasing use and demand for safety cases in new domains (automotive, maritime, nuclear) as well as developments in the use of AI in high risk systems (Myklebust et al., 2025).

As mentioned in Sect. 1.3, the structure of the safety plan chapters provides a clear link between the safety plan and the different parts of the safety case, facilitating an *incremental development of the safety plan into the safety case.* When developing a new safety system, we normally recommend that the safety engineering team develop an agile safety plan first, as described in this book. However, having a clear picture of the structure and the different parts of the final safety case from the project start is wise to ensure efficiency and synergies. We have therefore ensured that we have developed new chapters in the safety plan that corresponds to the new suggested parts of the safety case (see Table 1.1 for an overview of the different safety case parts).

To support a pragmatic and effective approach, we have incrementally developed the safety plan in several projects over several months. At the same time, we have developed drafts of relevant safety documentation that will become references in the safety case. See Annex A "Documents that are referenced in the safety case" and Annex B "AI Act Technical documentation and links to safety plan, safety case and named documents", which lists relevant documents that are referenced in both the safety plan and the safety case. After a few months or sometimes after a year or so, the safety plan is in some cases converted to a safety case. This is one of the reasons that in this book, we have tried to improve the link between the agile safety plan and the safety cases to be developed.

In most safety system certification projects, an existing system is improved. In several such systems, an impact analysis is performed. Then, based on the impact analysis and a check towards a safety plan template, the safety case is updated (Myklebust & Stålhane, 2021). See also Sect. 18.3.

While Sect. 1.3 provides an overview of how the different parts of the safety case are built up of input from the different safety plan chapters, Table 2.1 provides an overview of how the different safety plan chapters and sections relate to different parts of the safety case. This link is helpful when checking consistency and when we perform audits.

Table 2.1 Link between safety plan chapters and parts of the safety case

Agile safety plan chapters	Parts of the safety case (Myklebust et al. 2025)
2: Safety plan. Introduction, policy, and scope	Part 0: Introduction
3: DoS, ODD, and ConOps 3.1 Definition of the system (DoS) 3.2 Operational Design Domain (ODD) 3.3 Concept of Operation (ConOps)	Part 1: Definition of System Part 2: Operational Design Domain Part 3: Concept of Operation
4 Hardware	Part 1: Definition of System Part 6: Safety Management Report
5: Software and data	Part 1: Definition of System Part 6 Technical Safety Report
6: AI, XAI and SOTIF 6.1 AI 6.2 Explainable AI (XAI) 6.3 Safety of the Intended functionality (SOTIF)	Part 7: AI Safety Report
7: Stakeholders and organizations	Part 4: Quality Management Report
8: Compliance with regulations, FuSa, and AI standards	Part 5: Safety Management Report
9: Planning the safety activities: tests, analysis, scenarios, verifications, validations, and regression	Part 5: Safety Management Report
10: Lifecycles	Part 5: Safety Management Report Part 7: AI Safety Report
11: Tools, Programming Language, and Pre-existing SW	Part 5: Safety Management Report
12: Hazards and risks	Part 5: Safety Management Report
13: Requirements	Part 4: Quality Management Report Part 5: Safety Management Report
14: System design	Part 5: Safety Management Report
15: Documentation	Part 4: Quality Management Report
16: Human aspects	Part 8: Human Aspects and Oversight
17: Level of automation and autonomy	Part 7: AI Safety Report
18: Safety case, approval, and modifications	Part 5: Safety Management Report
19: Procurement and subcontractors	Part 4: Quality Management Report

2.2 The Strategy for Achieving Functional Safety

Objective

The objective is to define and implement a Functional Safety (FuSa) strategy for developing the product/system in question. This is to identify, analyse, and mitigate hazards throughout its lifecycle. With this strategy, developers should be able to adhere to the AI Act, and standards related to functional safety and AI. By implementing robust safety measures and fostering a safety-conscious culture, different stakeholders, such as operators and customers, are satisfied and contribute to system integrity. The end result of the development project is one or more safety cases following the product's lifecycle.

Information

In the context of a safety plan, a strategy refers to a plan aimed at achieving success in specific situations. For example, it may involve ensuring that a product is developed with only the necessary documentation required to obtain relevant approvals. Beyond outlining specific actions to take, the strategy should also include a set of guiding ideas and principles that the business organization has formally agreed upon. For instance, the management might decide to use the SafeScrum approach (Hanssen et al., 2018) for a particular development project or adopt a Minimum Viable Product (MVP) strategy as a key approach to expedite the development process. MVP is a development approach where a new product or service is created with just enough features to satisfy early customers and provide feedback for future development. This method allows companies to learn quickly, improve, and potentially enhance cash flow while minimizing risk, which is especially important for many start-ups. Additional safety and compliance standards must also be considered when developing an MVP.

Additionally, a relevant strategy could involve initially developing systems with limited risk, which are later intended to evolve into high risk systems, such as transitioning from an assistant system to a decision-making system.

This chapter is directly linked to the safety case section "Introduction". Company policies and strategies are sometimes referenced.

Requirements

These are part of the AI Act's generic requirements, such as Article 9, "Risk management system". They are also part of generic requirements in relevant functional safety and AI standards. If they are not sufficient, additional requirements have to be evaluated. Not all functional safety standards require a safety case, but this is the final goal of this agile safety plan

Agile Adaptations

Agile adaptations could be performed in all lifecycle parts, including a SafeScrum and DevOps approach.

Safety Plan Issues

The plan could include an MVP approach and explain how the MVP(s) certification requirements relate to the system's certification.

2.3 The Purpose, Scope, and Context of the Plan

Objective

The objective of this part of the agile safety plan is to seamlessly integrate FuSa principles with the project plan and software quality assurance plan for the product or system. The objective is to clearly define the development activities to be performed, often outlined in a business plan or contract. This involves aligning safety-related activities with project milestones and ensuring that safety considerations are embedded in every phase of the project lifecycle. The purpose, scope, and context specification should ensure that the plan includes all relevant domains, including the regions and countries where the product or system will be used.

Information

The scope often includes a reference to a contract. The contract could be between a railway operator and a manufacturer or an Original Equipment Manufacturer (OEM) and a manufacturer. Due to modularization and increased complexity, contract-based design (CBD) has also become more popular.

This chapter links to the safety case section "Introduction" (Myklebust et al., 2025).

The Safety Integrity Level (SIL) is a measure used to specify the necessary level of reliability and performance for safety systems in industries such as railway, automotive, and process industries. It ranks systems on a scale (SIL 1 to SIL 4) based on the required reduction in risk, with SIL 4 representing the highest level of safety. Different domains use SIL or similar terms, such ASIL (Automotive SIL) for automotive and DAL (Design Assurance Level) for aviation; see Table 2.2. The concept is widely used in safety-critical systems to ensure that these systems operate reliably under specified conditions, reducing the likelihood of dangerous failure. For instance, SIL 4 systems are expected to have an extremely low likelihood of failure, especially in high risk environments.

Requirements

This is part of the AI Act's generic requirements, such as Article 9, "Risk management system". Generic requirements in safety and AI standards and which standards are relevant are often listed. In addition, the relevant SIL or ASIL, to be achieved are mentioned; see Table 2.2. When incorporating AI functionality, it is also important to make sure that complying with standards is sufficient; see Chap. 8. One should, if necessary, specify other relevant requirements to ensure that the EU AI Act is satisfied.

Agile Adaptations

The agile community "embraces change". Thus, we may expect changes in the project's scope several times during an agile project. In the development project, scope changes, including scope creep, should be handled through change control. Normally, the safety requirements are more stable than the other requirements.

Table 2.2 Safety integrity levels

Domain	Domain-specific safety levels				
IEC 61508 Generic safety	NA	SIL1	SIL2	SIL3	SIL4
IEC 61511 Process industry	NA	SIL1	SIL2	SIL3	SIL4
EN 5012X Railway EN 50716 Railway	Basic Integrity	SIL1	SIL2	SIL3	SIL4
ISO 26262 Automotive	ASIL-A	ASIL-B	ASIL-C	ASIL-D	NA
DO-178 Aviation	DAL-E	DAL-D	DAL-C	DAL-B	DAL-A
DO-278 Aviation	AL6	AL5	AL3	AL2	AL1
ISO 13849 Machine	a	b and c	d	e	NA
IEC 62061 Machine	NA	SIL1	SIL2	SIL3	NA

2.4 Limitations and Assumptions Made

Objective
The limitations and assumptions that will be included in the safety case should be planned for and presented concisely, transparently, and understandable.

Information
You will often find that limitations and assumptions about the system are mentioned in the safety case introduction. However, these limitations and assumptions might also appear in different parts of the safety case and its references. It is important for the relevant stakeholders to review these limitations and assumptions. If needed, they should be updated or consolidated into a single chapter in future versions of the documents to ensure clarity and consistency.

There are several ways to convey the specific assumptions underlying a safety case, and Goal Structuring Notation (GSN) is one of them. In GSN an ""Assumption" is a core element used to declare unsubstantiated statements considered true for the argument (ACWG, 2021). These are critical for building claims and strategies, providing transparency, and allowing proper validation. Assumptions applied to goals and strategies define the context within which they are valid, ensuring the argument acknowledges these conditions. This is to ensure that the argument is robust and comprehensively documented.

This chapter of the safety plan is linked to the "Introduction" chapter in the safety case as suggested by Myklebust et al. (2025).

Requirements
This is part of the AI Act's generic requirements, such as Article 9, "Risk Management System", and Article 13, "Transparency and provision of information to deployers".

In IEC 61508-1:2010, "assumptions" are mentioned as part of e.g.

- Requirements regarding demand rates and failure rates during operation and maintenance.
- Risk reduction measures

In UL 4600:2023, "limitations" are mentioned as a possible pitfall related to e.g.

- Taking credit for conformance to a standard.
- Unit testing of large SW units and missing defects due to limitations and observability

In UL 4600:2023, "assumptions" are mentioned as a possible pitfall related to e.g.

- Independent failures are prone to over-stating sensor fusion effectiveness

Environmental limitations should normally be presented in the SC or one or more of the references. In addition, limitations and assumptions are almost always presented in the related SC-es; see Sect. 18.3. Be aware of assumptions that are not clearly identified.

The ISO 26262 series was originally intended for passenger vehicles, and corresponding assumptions are embedded in the formulation of ASIL-D requirements (UL4600:2023).

ISO 21448:2022 includes requirements on safety of the intended functionality (SOTIF) including aspects such as performance limitation.

A high level of AI explainability prevents unpredictable behaviour but can reduce decision quality due to current technology limitations. ISO/IEC 5469:2024 includes information related to the limitation of test coverage.

Agile Adaptation

Agile adaptations can be applied throughout the entire product lifecycle, including using approaches such as SafeScrum and DevOps. Agile practices should be tailored to meet functional safety requirements when necessary. For example, adopting an MVP approach allows for early delivery with limited features, which can be expanded and refined over time as part of a continuous improvement process. This flexibility enables organizations to respond effectively to changes while maintaining a focus on safety.

Safety Plan Issues

Testing, analysis, and simulations often include assumptions about the environment in which the system is used, which may become invalidated over time. Therefore, the limitations and assumptions need to be kept up to date and consulted when planning tests, analysis, and simulations.

Remember the relevant issues and requirements mentioned above. Include all limitations and assumptions in a dedicated chapter in the SC.

Chapter 3
Definition of the System, Operational Design Domain, and Concept of Operation

This chapter consists of three section outlining how a description of a safety-critical system should be provided. First, we elaborate on how the *Definition of the System* (DoS) should be provided, ensuring a detailed description of the system for which the safety case is being presented. Next, we elaborate on how the environment surrounding the safety-critical system should be accounted for through a detailed description of the *Operational Design Domain* (ODD). Lastly, we outline how the *Concept of Operation* (ConOps) bridges the description made of the DoS and the ODD by addressing the different types of users and modes of operation of the system. By taking all these three aspects into account, a comprehensive description of the safety-critical system in its operational use should be accounted for.

3.1 Definition of the System (DoS)

Objective
This section's objective is to precisely define and provide references to the system, subsystem, Minimum Viable Products (MVP), or equipment to which the safety case shall refer, including the version numbers and modification status of all requirements, design, and application documentation.

Information
The first sections in the safety case are the DoS and the ODD. The DoS shall give a complete and detailed description of the *system* for which the safety case is being presented, while the ODD shall give a complete description of the system's *operating environment* (see Sect. 3.2). The DoS is important for hazard and risk work. Consequently, it is important to have a good description of the DoS in the early safety phases. In several of our development projects, we have also experienced that an improved DoS has led to better overall understanding by the development team working with software and AI.

© The Author(s) 2025
T. Myklebust et al., *The AI Act and The Agile Safety Plan*, SpringerBriefs in
Computer Science, https://doi.org/10.1007/978-3-031-80504-2_3

In the automotive domain, two crucial elements are important parts of the DoS. The dynamic driving task (DDT) and object and event detection and response (OEDR). They are an integral part of DoS because they define the system's capabilities in handling the vehicle's driving operations. OEDR is part of the DDT as it detects objects (vehicles, pedestrians, obstacles) and responds appropriately (slowing down, stopping, or manoeuvring). Regulation 2022/1426 (REG. 31) includes a comprehensive definition: 4. 'dynamic driving task ('DDT')' *means all real-time operational functions and tactical functions required to operate the vehicle, excluding strategic functions such as trip scheduling and selection of destinations and waypoints and including without limitation the following subtasks: (a) Lateral vehicle motion control via steering (operational); (b) Longitudinal vehicle motion control via acceleration and deceleration (operational); (c) Monitoring the driving environment via object and event detection, recognition, classification, and response preparation (operational and tactical); (d) Object and event response execution (operational and tactical); (e) Manoeuvre planning (tactical); (f) Enhancing conspicuity via lighting, sounding the horn, signalling, gesturing, etc. (tactical).*

This chapter has a direct link to the safety plan and the safety case chapter with the same title.

Requirements

Relevant requirements to the DoS are presented in the AI Act Annex IV, "Technical documentation referred to in Article 11(1)". This Annex also requires a description of tools provided by third parties. This is often presented in one of the references in the safety case, for instance, the "tool validation document". The best current descriptions of requirements for the DoS are presented in railway domain standards EN 50129:2018 and EN 50126–1:2017 Annex D "Guidance on system definition" which can be used in combination with *The Agile Safety Case* book by Myklebust and Stålhane (2018). In EN 50129:2018 (page 43) DoS is described as follows: *"This shall precisely define or reference the system, subsystem or equipment to which the Safety Case refers, including version numbers and modification status of all requirements, design and application documentation. When the Safety Case is issued or re-issued due to a change or reconfiguration, a delivery sheet or a release note reporting the complete configuration shall be referenced here. The delivery sheet or release note shall also list the current and previous versions of all the modified products and applications."* Other safety standards, like IEC 61508 and ISO 26262, only mention this topic without any guidance.

Agile Adaptation

A first edition of the DoS should be established already at the concept phase and then incrementally developed to ensure that it is a good basis for hazard and risk analysis. Safety systems are often divided into several components and products, and it has become increasingly popular to develop a system by first developing one or more MVPs. MVPs are integral to agile methodologies and relevant for the DoS because they facilitate early and frequent feedback, reduce risk, promote flexibility, encourage continuous improvement, deliver early value, focus on core functionality, and validate assumptions.

Safety Plan Issues

When developing new products, we often start with a basic version that could be considered a variant of an MVP. This initial version helps us test the concept and gather feedback. However, there are important certification requirements that must be met for the MVP and the final product. The certification requirements can be reduced for the MVP, depending on the product and domain. For example, the first MVP might function as an assistance system offering suggestions or support to users. At this stage, the certification process may be less stringent. As the product evolves, it could develop into an autonomous decision-making system, operating without the need for human intervention. Such systems usually require a more rigorous certification process because they put a higher level of responsibility on the manufacturer. Based on our experience, it is crucial to clearly define and describe the MVP or final product early in the development process. Doing so helps ensure that everyone involved understands the goals and requirements, which can streamline the development and certification process.

3.2 Operational Design Domain (ODD)

Objective

The physical environment and the system environment—the ODD—are important for hazard and safety analysis since they will decide the consequences of any failed functionality. The education and experience of the system's users are crucial, as they influence how users manage unexpected events and determine the amount of information required for their actions. The ODD can be given a wide or narrow interpretation depending on the purpose. The choice of interpretation may change during the system's lifetime.

Information

This section contains information and links to the safety case chapter and relevant documents to be referenced. We also give some basic definitions and references to other relevant book chapters. An important part is the links between the computer, environment, users, and software which is shown in Fig. 3.1.

Put in a simple but general way, environment is anything that

- Is external to the system we are developing but must be considered during development.
- When changed, should initiate a change to the system under consideration. The environment will depend on the system's intended purpose but will always include.

  - Computer Hardware, Operating System and Libraries, or Commercial Off-the-Shelf (COTS) software—if used.
  - Users' purpose, experience, and education.

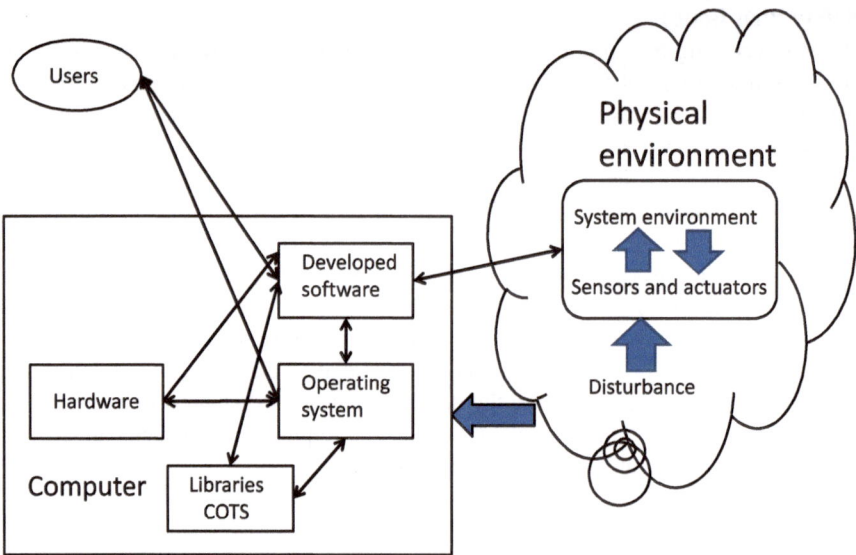

Fig. 3.1 The connection between the computer, environment, users, and software

- The physical environment of the system is supposed to control and operate in. For an Autonomous Vehicle this is a description of the roads and the Autonomous Vehicle's hardware, software, and operating system. For a system controlling an industrial process it includes the process, its equipment, and the factory floor.

The challenges related to ODD increase when we use artificial intelligence; examples are

- AI systems often rely on multiple sensors to build a complete understanding of their environment. Failures or misalignment in sensor data can lead to operational errors.
- AI systems can use transfer learning to generalize knowledge from one environment to another. However, transferring learned behaviour from one ODD to a broader or different one (e.g. from urban to rural driving) without introducing safety risks is a complex task.
- Data drift occurs when the distribution of runtime input data deviates from that used during the model's training phase. This can lead to a deterioration in performance, including potential safety risks, especially when the model is deployed in critical applications. See also clause 8.4.2.1 in ISO/IEC 5469:2024.
- Concept drift in the relationship between the input variables and the model's output, often associated with changes in the underlying data distribution. This phenomenon can cause a model's predictions to become less reliable over time if not addressed. See also clause 8.4.2.2 in ISO/IEC 5469:2024.

- Safe exploration arises when safety constraints are imposed during data collection and training, limiting the range of data used for training and potentially restricting the ability to learn from "unsafe" scenarios. Safe exploration is crucial not only for physical entities such as service robots or unmanned aerial systems but also for software agents, including those using reinforcement learning, which must carefully explore their operational environments while adhering to safety constraints.
- AI systems can encounter ambiguous situations where it is unclear how they should behave (e.g. a roadblock without clear signs on how to proceed).

The requirements, the environment description, the safety plan, and the safety case are mutually dependent. The requirements and the environment are linked through users, assumptions, required functionality, and safety. The safety plan—what we should do—and the safety case—what we need to prove—are also dependent on each other. Both will be living documents, and changes to one will lead to changes in the other.

Requirements

The requirements of the system to be developed and its intended operating environment combined will give the requirements for the ODD description. It is practical to split the ODD description into three parts; see also Fig. 3.2:

- Static part—parts that will be unchanged for a long time—Scenery in Fig. 3.2
- Dynamic part—parts that will change over time due to use—Dynamic elements in Fig. 3.2
- Environmental conditions—external influences on the static part and dynamic part (e.g. weather)—Environmental conditions in Fig. 3.2

Most application areas have made no attempts to standardize the ODD description. The automobile is an exception, as shown below BSI PAS 1883:2020 "ODD".

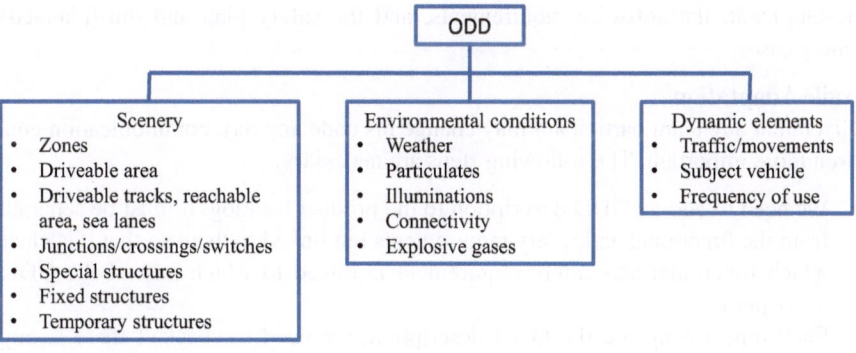

Fig. 3.2 Top level taxonomy with ODD attributes

The three components of an ODD are explained in the list below together with some examples:

- Scenery—the static parts—will only change in a long-time perspective, months or years. Are affected by long-time planning—e.g. construction work.
  This part is used to describe roads, built infrastructure, houses, etc. If necessary, it might be divided into different zones. The type of zones will depend on the type of static parts. Examples of traffic zones:

  - Roundabouts
  - Crossings
  - Bicycle lanes

- Examples of university building zones:

  - Auditoriums
  - Corridors
  - Offices

- Dynamic elements—may change from one minute to the next—e.g. change of traffic. This can usually not be predicted.
  Examples of traffic dynamics:

  - Traffic jam
  - High-priority vehicles—e.g. fire trucks

- Environmental conditions—may change during the day—e.g. weather conditions.
  Examples of environmental conditions:

  - Heavy rain
  - Slippery road

For any software development project, the developer, the assessor, and the customer need to agree on an ODD description and the connection between software development, the software requirements, and the safety plan and the (planned) safety case.

Agile Adaptation

Given that any team participant may change his code any day, communication gets even more important. The following steps are necessary:

- We need to add an ODD description to the product backlog. It must be separate from the functional and safety requirements but linked to them so that it is clear which functional and safety requirement is linked to which part of the ODD description.
- Each time we update the ODD description, we need to check if there is any requirement, either in the backlog or already processed that needs to be updated. Changes to the environment or our understanding of it may influence our safety analysis. This requires that the ODD connections are kept in the code.

- At each daily stand-up, we need to ask an extra question: will what you did yesterday or what you will do today influence our description or expectations of the system's environment?

Safety Plan Issues

During software development, it is important to document and trace all decisions and assumptions that are related to the system's environment. This is important for management, assessors, and customers and for later updates. It is also important for living documents, such as safety analysis, safety cases, and the safety plan. In addition, the following question should be addressed in each stand-up meeting? "Are you planning to do anything that will influence our environment assumptions?" It might be necessary to involve the alongside engineering team here. Therefore, to be on the safe side we must ensure that:

- All assumptions plus their dependencies and consequences/decisions for the current project are documented. This process must start when the project starts. Beware—our understanding, also of the environment, will increase as the project moves towards completion.
- The project establishes traces between assumptions/decisions and the project's safety plan and the software product—including documentation, training programme, and tests.
- If artificial intelligence is used as part of the system, we need to control changes to the training environment—see Chaps. 6 and 10.
- Possible changes to the environment or changes to our understanding of the environment are an issue at each daily stand-up meeting.

3.3   Concept of Operation (ConOps)

Objective

A ConOps shall be based on both the envisioned (planned) system (DoS) and the ODD. It should also describe the types of users and their modes of operation. In addition, it should help to prioritize conflicting needs among user groups. The objective is to ensure safe, efficient, and reliable operations. With all of this information available, it is straightforward to do a hazard analysis and—based on the hazard analysis—to start developing a safety case.

Information

The concept of operations should describe the AI system, its purpose, and how it is intended to operate in a real-world environment. It typically includes high-level requirements, the types of users, and their interactions with the system. A key objective of ConOps is to ensure safe, efficient, and reliable operations by addressing potential hazards and conflicting user needs. This foundational document is essential in aligning the system's design with its intended use and helps in risk analysis and safety assessments.

Requirements

The AI Act's "intended purpose" is closely linked to the ConOps. The AI Act often uses sentences such as "intended purpose", "intended to be used", or "performs as intended". An "intended purpose" refers to the intended use of an AI system as defined by the provider, outlined in the instructions for use, promotional and sales materials, statements, and technical documentation. This also includes the specific context the system is intended for and conditions for use.

Often, the terms "intended use" and "intended purpose" are used interchangeably (van Leeuwen et al., 2024). This is for instance the case in the Medical Device Regulation. Here, "intended purpose" is defined as follows: "intended purpose means the use for which a device is intended according to the data supplied by the manufacturer on the label, in the instructions for use or in promotional or sales materials or statements and as specified by the manufacturer in the clinical evaluation" (van Leeuwen et al., 2024).

The ConOps concept is mentioned neither in the IEC 61508, the ISO 26262, nor in the ISO/IEC TR 5469. However, work has been done to include the ConOps in ISO 26262—see [2]: "To extend the fundamental concepts of ISO 26262 to operationally complex systems, the proposed methodology incorporates a Concept of Operations (ConOps) and safe state behaviours into the standard ISO 26262 work product structure".

A ConOps shall describe

- The envisioned (planned) system

    - Rational—who wants the system and why—for what purpose
    - High-level requirements—including relevant laws, regulations, and standards
    - Assumptions made
    - The AI training set(s)
    - Conflicting needs among the user groups and how to prioritize them

- The types of users—e.g. their jobs, knowledge, and training
- The system's modes of operation
- The system's validation process, including software, hardware, and the ODD
- Safety and security—including a hazard and risk analysis
- Required portability
- Relevant project information

Some persons claim that safe behaviour is part of ConOps. However, when extending ISO 26262, the authors use the statement "Concept of Operations (ConOps) **and** safe state behaviours"—see Dawson & Garikapati (2021). Safety analysis is handled in another chapter. Here we will only provide two examples of early, high-level safety requirements:

- Seaworthiness—maritime concept for the measure of a vessel's suitability for safe operations while underway
- Airworthiness—the fitness of an aircraft for flight in all conditions for which it has been designed and to which it may therefore be exposed

Safety Plan Issues

Whether we use AI or not, the challenge for ConOps is that things may change over time and often in an unpredictable way. Agility was developed just to deal with such changes. This applies to requirements, users, assumptions, and the operating environment—the ODD. As a consequence of this, if any of the issues in the list in the section above change, we also need to consider the rest of the issues.

The first and most important thing when it comes to planning for the ConOps is simple: "Understand your market". This includes what the system shall be used for, in which environment and by whom.

The next important thing to remember is "Prepare for change". Since the ConOps spans the whole product and development process, there are several important relationships. We will just look at a few:

- Requirements may change over time, together with our understanding of the requirements' implication for our system, its use, and the related hazards and the safety case.
- The user group may change.
- Our understanding of the ODD or the ODD itself may change. This will influence the requirements, the hazards, and thus the safety case.

"Prepare for change" has some important consequences. We need bidirectional links between any two documents where information is shared, or one influences the other. For example, if the system's purpose is changed (e.g. extended), we will, at minimum, need to rerun the AI training, do a new hazard analysis, and make a new safety case.

Chapter 4
Hardware/Chip

While software development is the main focus of this book, we cannot ignore hardware when discussing AI. Hardware plays a major role in how well AI works. Even the smartest software cannot function properly without strong, fast, and capable hardware such as computers, processors, and chips. Therefore, while the book is about writing and developing AI programs, we also need to include information about the hardware that runs them because it is crucial for AI's performance and success.

Objective

The objective is to evaluate hardware and, when relevant, align advancements in chip technology with robust software development practices, ensuring safe hardware (HW) and software (SW) integration. In the rapidly evolving field of AI high risk systems, chips and sensors play a critical role. While standard hardware components may not require detailed inclusion in the safety plan, custom-made or customer-adapted hardware, such as Field-Programmable Gate Arrays (FPGAs) or standard hardware with embedded software, must be thoroughly analysed. This includes the development, validation, and updates, planned or unplanned, to ensure comprehensive safety management. FPGAs are flexible computer chips that can be customized after manufacturing to perform specific tasks. Unlike regular chips with fixed functions, FPGAs can be reprogrammed to adapt to different needs, making them useful in industries that require tailored solutions, such as AI or telecommunications. This adaptability allows for faster processing and efficient use of resources in specialized applications.

Information

Safety chips are critical components in many high risk AI systems because they help ensure that the system operates reliably and securely. These chips are designed to detect and respond to system faults or errors, automatically triggering safety mechanisms like shutting down or switching to backup modes. They also enhance cybersecurity by protecting the system from unauthorized access or malicious attacks. In

T. Myklebust et al., *The AI Act and The Agile Safety Plan*, SpringerBriefs in Computer Science, https://doi.org/10.1007/978-3-031-80504-2_4

industries like healthcare or autonomous driving, these chips are crucial to prevent dangerous failures and make AI systems safer and more trustworthy.

This section has a link to the "assurance of correct hardware functionality" chapter of the Technical Safety Report (TSR). While software may change once a month, hardware is often not changed more than once a year in several domains, such as the automotive domain.

The following advice from Myklebust and Stålhane (2018) is still relevant and adapted to this book: If HW development is included, an EMC (Electro Magnetic Compatibility) compliance plan should be referenced to or included in the safety plan.

EMC is still important and difficult to satisfy for the manufacturers that develop HW. One of the authors has experienced, since the issue of the EMC directive 89/336/EEC in 1989, that more than 90% of the products fail in at least one test the first time EMC tests are performed (Myklebust & Stålhane, 2018). This has been more challenging when using normative EMC standards listed in functional standards than when complying only with harmonized standards listed as part of the EMC directive. For more information, see Chap. 9.

The EMC directive came into force in 1992 and has been mandatory for CE marking of electronic/electrical products since 1 January 1996. Start-ups and other companies that are new to certifications should learn from the EMCD (EMC Directive) guide (European Commission, 2018).

The automotive industry has several existing standards for functional safety and AI, with more being developed. Using these international standards, also for other domains (Okoh & Myklebust, 2024a), is important for creating cost-effective and safe designs. See also Sect. 2.3 regarding standards.

Requirements

The AI Act does not directly specify hardware specifications. Compliance with the high risk AI requirements involves ensuring that the hardware supports the system's functional needs, such as transparency, human oversight, and data logging. For more information, see Chap. 8.

EU AI Act Annex IV, "Technical documentation", lists relevant HW information that must be provided for high risk systems. Other relevant documents are listed in Annex A of this book.

Production of high risk systems is of crucial importance. See Fig. 4.1. This is weakly described in IEC 61508, but the ISO 26262 series has one standard that includes this important topic. The production of safety systems, as outlined in ISO 26262-7:2018, focuses on ensuring that functional safety is maintained throughout the production phase. This involves strict planning of production processes, adherence to safety-related special characteristics, and the use of appropriate tools and control measures. The production process must include safety considerations, such as identifying potential failures and implementing measures to mitigate them, ensuring that each step of the production maintains the integrity of the safety-related elements to achieve the desired functional safety objectives.

Hardware requirements are presented in several functional safety standards:

Fig. 4.1 Production of detectors at Autronica Fire and Security AS

Generic safety standards:

1. IEC 61508-2:2010 Generic hardware requirements
2. Draft IEC TS 61508-2-1 Functional safety of electrical/electronic/programmable electronic safety-related systems Part 2-1: Requirements for complex semiconductors

Railway:

3. EN 50129:2018 railway

   • Components with Inherent Physical Properties—see EN 50129:2018, C.4 "*Procedure for components with inherent physical properties*"

Automotive:

4. ISO 26262-5:2018 Automotive hardware requirements
5. ISO 26262-11 Semiconductors

Functional safety and AI:

6. ISO/IEC TR 5469:2024 FuSa and AI. Section 8.6 AI HW issues

Regarding the maritime domain, Directive 2014/90/EU presents requirements for marine equipment, and the Implementing Regulation (EU) 2023/1667 lists relevant standards and includes links to IMO and SOLAS requirements.

Agile Adaptation

Hardware can be developed using an agile approach, allowing for faster and more flexible updates compared to traditional methods. FPGAs enable hardware customization after manufacturing, making it easier to adapt to changing requirements without the need to redesign the entire system. Traditionally, hardware is planned on a yearly cycle, as seen in car manufacturers' annual updates to new models. For instance, when a sensor is upgraded in a car, it might also require new software to integrate the data from that sensor into the vehicle's system, such as in sensor fusion, which combines inputs from multiple sources. Additionally, improving the ODD— the conditions under which the system operates—may necessitate adding or modifying sensors to meet new performance standards or safety requirements.

Safety Plan Issues

Including a good purchase plan and process is often of great importance when considering hardware products to be included in high risk AI systems. It is important to ask for relevant information early on, like a safety manual (Myklebust & Stålhane, 2022). Also, considerations relating to periodic chip shortages make it important to establish contact and contracts with suppliers at an early point in several instances.

Chapter 5
Software and Data

This chapter first outlines why software and data are relevant to consider when developing safety-critical applications and which requirements need to be considered in this context. We consider both the software that companies buy and the software they develop themselves, but also pay attention to the software already present within the hardware that is in use. The chapter also provides a section on data, pointing out some key aspects relevant to consider in the context of developing AI and safety-critical systems.

5.1 Software

Objective
When we select software—whether we buy it or develop it—we need to be able to assess safety and related risks. In order to get a good understanding of the software's safety we need to consider the whole development process—design, development, testing, and quality assurance.

Information
First and foremost, we need to consider the three types of software involved in most safety-critical applications:

- Software already inside the hardware we buy—e.g. the operating system of a laptop.
- Software we buy from other companies, i.e. COTS—see Chap. 19. This usually also includes software that is part of equipment that we buy, e.g. sensors and actuators.
- Software that we develop—mostly system applications related.

All of these types of software may introduce hazards—the two first categories mainly because they might have been made to other requirements, other ODDs, or

© The Author(s) 2025
T. Myklebust et al., *The AI Act and The Agile Safety Plan*, SpringerBriefs in
Computer Science, https://doi.org/10.1007/978-3-031-80504-2_5

other processes. The complexity of SW development increases the risk of human error, coding flaws, or design oversights, which can lead to vulnerabilities or failures in real-world operations. See also Chap. 19, "Procurement and subcontractors".

Section 5.1 has a link to the chapter on "Assurance of correct software functionality of the safety case".

See also Chap. 11 "Tools, programming languages, and pre-existing software" of this book.

Requirements

The AI Act includes several requirements related to software, e.g. copy from parts of Annex IV Technical

- 1b—"The technical documentation referred to in Article 11(1) shall contain at least the following information, as applicable to the relevant AI system … how the AI system interacts with, or can be used to interact with, hardware or software, including with other AI systems, that are not part of the AI system itself, where applicable"
- 2c—"A detailed description of the elements of the AI system and of the process for its development, including … the description of the system architecture explaining how software components build on or feed into each other and integrate into the overall processing; the computational resources used to develop, train, test and validate the AI system"

The necessary software safety requirements are presented in, e.g., these functional safety standards:

- IEC 61508, part 3-2010, Generic functional safety standard for software development
- ISO 26262, part 6-2018—Automotive
- EN 50716:2023 Railway Applications—Requirements for software development

Agile Adaptations

Due to the increasing digitalization of safety-critical systems, software and data are critical components in most businesses. Thus, in an ever-changing world, software is bound to change. As a result of adapting an agile approach we are prepared for changes and should be able to change data and software in a controlled way without large problems. The most important thing is to make sure that *all dependencies* between developed software and software delivered as part of external equipment are documented so that we know what is dependent on what. This will again influence our planning process and the safety case—if component X is changed, we know what software should be updated.

See also Chap. 9—Lifecycles, which describes SafeScrum—a version of Scrum that is specialized for the development of safety-critical systems.

Safety Plan Issues

The most important action when making plans is to remember the agile slogan "Prepare/plan for change". In many safety-critical systems, considerable software is delivered from companies outside of our control. Thus, our plans for change must include answers to questions such as "What do we need to change if/when company X delivers a new version of their sensors?" The same holds for any other change involving the ODD.

There are more and more—and better and better—tools available that can generate high-quality software based on, e.g., UML diagrams (Kundu et al., 2013) or state charts (Jakimi & Elkoutbi, 2009). This trend will increase with the increasing use of AI. Since this makes it easier to update software, it will make it easier to cope with changes in the system's environment. However, it might also, as a consequence, lead to more frequent updates from external software providers, which implies more hazards.

5.2   Data

Objective
The objective is to plan for data preparation, gather relevant data, turn them into safe data, and develop them into safety insight and safety actions.

Information
While data is defined as part of the software in IEC 61508-4:2010 "*3.2.5 software: intellectual creation comprising the programs, procedures, data, rules and any associated documentation pertaining to the operation of a data processing system*", data safety is not defined in any safety standards. However, data safety is thoroughly described in the Data safety guidance (DSIWG, 2024). Based on this, we define data safety as "*The process of ensuring that data used in safety-related systems is accurately managed, controlled, and processed to prevent hazards and harm.*"

In safety-critical systems, data are used in several ways: as configuration information, input to and output from algorithms—e.g. input from sensors and resulting output to operators and actuators, and data used to calibrate instruments. In some cases, data will also have value as part of a machine learning process—MLOps (Machine Learning OPs), using the same ideas as DevOps (Meritt, 2020). In addition, safety-critical systems may be used to store important data—e.g. personal information. As a consequence of this, the safety plan must contain information on how to protect critical data. Data will change because the environment changes or because one or more applications change. Thus, we need a process in place for safely changing data.

This chapter is directly linked to the safety case chapter with the same title. Relevant documents are listed in Annex A of this book.

Requirements
The AI Act includes several requirements related to data, e.g. as stated in Annex IV Technical documentation, "*(d) where relevant, the data requirements in terms of datasheets describing the training methodologies and techniques and the training data sets used, including a general description of the data sets, information about*

their provenance, scope and main characteristics; how data was obtained and selected; labelling procedures (e.g. for supervised learning), data cleaning method- ologies (e.g. outliers detection)".

When working with data, it is essential to comply with the EU Regulation on Fair Access to and Use of Data, specifically the Data Act (EU 2023/2854), which entered into force on 11 January 2024. This legislation establishes clear rules on data access and sharing, promoting fairness across data market participants while safeguarding the interests of those who invest in data-generation technologies. For more detailed guidance, see the *Data Act explained* (EU, 2024g) and the *Frequently Asked Questions* (EU, 2024h).

Data requirements are presented in the functional safety standards presented in Table 5.1.

Table 5.1 FuSa standards, including comments and recommendations regarding data

Functional safety standards	Comments and recommendations
1. IEC 61508-3:2010 Annex G (informative) Guidance for tailoring lifecycles associated with data-driven systems.	• The current edition is weak when it comes to data • Copy from the standard *"Many systems are written in two parts. One part provides the underlying system capability. The other part adapts the system to the specific requirements of the intended application.* *The application part may be written in the form of data, which configures the system part. This is termed "data driven" in this Annex"* • We recommend to also using the Data safety guideline (STD6)
2. IEC 61508-3 draft 2024 Annex G (informative) Data-driven systems	• Annex G will be improved in the next edition of IEC 61508-3 but is still weak in the current 2024 draft • We recommend to also using the Data safety guideline (STD6)
3. EN 50716:2023 Railway Applications—Requirements for software development	Chapter 8 *Development of application data: systems configured by application data* is relevant for application data; in other cases we recommend Data safety guideline (STD6)
4. ISO 26262-6:2018 Automotive software requirements	This standard includes several data requirements but does not include a separate chapter or annex that gives a good overview of the data requirements. For simple cases, this standard seems to be acceptable, but if having a more complex data system, we recommend also using the Data safety guideline (STD6)
5. ISO/IEC TR 5469:2024 FuSa and AI.	This TR includes five relevant data chapters when developing AI systems: 9.3.2 "Relationship between data distributions and HARA" 9.3.3 Data preparation and model-level validation and verification 9.3.6 Mitigating techniques for data size limitation 10.3.5 "Protection of the data and parameters"
6. BSI PAS 1882:2021 Data collection and management for automated vehicle trials—Specification	The purpose of this PAS data management as part of vehicle trials. It is one of the few standards that mention incident investigation

Agile Adaptations

Due to the increasing digitalization of safety systems, e.g. autonomous systems, data have become far more important. Relevant data are

- Configuration data: Railway control systems and air traffic control systems typically have large amounts of data to adapt the generic software to the given control area. For railway applications, see EN 50716:2023
- Geographical Data. Similar to the example above but derived from external sources (e.g. nautical chart data). Used in, e.g., autonomous and semi-autonomous vehicles. The safety standards in the table above have not specifically mentioned geographical data challenges.
- Datasets imported automatically or entered manually. For example, health informatics data
- Real-time data derived from sensors. This is normally part of the SRS and as such addressed indirectly by IEC 61508:2010.

Safety Plan Issues

When using data to develop high risk systems, it is essential to address several topics. Firstly, data protection measures must be established to safeguard critical and personal information used and stored in safety-critical systems. Secondly, a rigorous process for safely managing changes to data is necessary due to potential modifications in the environment or applications. Additionally, adherence to data requirements outlined in standards such as IEC 61508, ISO 26262, and the AI Act is crucial, particularly regarding training data, labelling procedures, and data cleaning methodologies. Ensuring proper validation and verification of data distributions and the relationship with hazard and risk analysis (HARA) is also vital. Finally, as systems become increasingly digitalized, the integration of configuration data, geographical data, and real-time sensor data must be managed carefully to maintain system safety and functionality.

Chapter 6
Artificial Intelligence (AI)

This chapter first provides a section on artificial intelligence (AI) in high risk systems, giving an overview over the current progress in standards relating to this topic. Next, a section addresses explainable AI (XAI) both as a technical concept and as a concept that has evident human and organizational sides to it. Lastly, a section on the concept of safety of intended functionality (SOTIF) is provided as it addresses safety in AI-driven systems, especially autonomous vehicles. This approach helps mitigate risks from functional insufficiencies in AI algorithms, making it vital for deploying AI safely in high risk areas.

6.1 Safe Artificial Intelligence (AI)

Objective
The objective of this part of the safety plan is to provide guidelines for the safe integration of AI technologies in safety-related systems. It aims to foster awareness of the properties, functional safety risk factors, available functional safety methods, and potential constraints associated with AI technologies. The plan should outline a structured approach to ensure that AI systems comply with existing functional safety standards and address the unique challenges posed by AI, including machine learning. By implementing this plan, developers can mitigate risks and ensure the reliability and safety of AI-driven safety functions.

Information
This chapter has a direct link to the safety case (SC) chapter with the same title. Other relevant documents depend on the product or system to be developed and, e.g., the classes presented in ISO/IEC TR 5469:2024.

It is worth noting that the ISO/PAS 8800:2024-12 Road Vehicles, "Safety and artificial intelligence," has recently been issued. This pas includes many work products that significantly impact the field of AI safety for road vehicles.

© The Author(s) 2025
T. Myklebust et al., *The AI Act and The Agile Safety Plan*, SpringerBriefs in Computer Science, https://doi.org/10.1007/978-3-031-80504-2_6

'AI system' means, according to the AI Act, *a machine-based system that is designed to operate with varying levels of autonomy and that may exhibit **adaptiveness after deployment**, and that, for explicit or implicit objectives, infers, from the input it receives, how to generate outputs such as predictions, content, recommendations, or decisions that can influence physical or virtual environments.*

Although adaptiveness after deployment is an important part of the "AI system" definition, the EU AI Act does not impose specific requirements directly tied to "adaptiveness after deployment" as a stand-alone feature. However, the concept of adaptiveness is integral to the definition of AI systems in the Act, which states that AI systems may exhibit adaptive behaviours after deployment. General requirements are related to risk management and to ensuring that AI systems consistently meet safety, transparency, accuracy, and robustness criteria throughout their lifecycle. See also Chaps. 8 and 10, and Sect. 18.3. And observe the definition of "substantial modification" in the AI Act. The definition is repeated in Annex B of this book.

Requirements

The rapid integration of AI into safety-critical systems necessitates robust standards to ensure functional safety. The European Union's AI Act underscores the importance of developing such standards by setting high-level safety requirements for AI systems. However, the development of detailed, mature AI standards remains a challenge, as they are still incomplete and immature compared to standards in other domains; see also Sect. 1.2. Below, we present relevant AI standards (see also Chap. 8).

Generally, the AI Act emphasizes transparency, while standards focus more on explainability. ISO/IEC TR 5469:2024 provides guidelines on ensuring the functional safety of AI systems. It addresses the unique risks associated with AI, such as unpredictability and lack of transparency, by recommending comprehensive risk assessment and mitigation strategies. The standard emphasizes the need for continuous monitoring and validation of AI systems throughout their lifecycle to maintain safety integrity. The TR also includes an annex that analyses the applicability of techniques and measures presented in IEC 61508-3:2010 Annexes A and B to AI technology elements.

None of the standards and documents listed below are referenced in ISO/IEC TR 5469:2024. ISO TR 4804:2020. "Road vehicles: Safety and cybersecurity for automated driving systems. Design, verification, and validation". This document explains how to create and test self-driving car systems using safety guidelines. It covers how to build these systems with safety and cybersecurity in mind, and how to check and confirm that the systems work correctly. The focus is on cars with advanced self-driving features (levels 3 and 4; see Chap. 17). It also discusses how to keep these systems secure while also making sure they are safe. This standard will be replaced by ISO/CD TS 5083.

ISO 24089:2023 "Road Vehicles—Software Update Engineering" standard focuses on software update engineering for road vehicles but can be adapted to other systems and domains, offering guidelines to ensure secure and effective software updates. It outlines how organizations should plan, develop, and implement updates for vehicles and electronic control units (ECUs), emphasizing the importance of maintaining vehicle safety and cybersecurity throughout the process. The standard provides steps for verifying, validating, and approving software updates before they are deployed. It also covers how to manage software update campaigns, including communication with users, handling update dependencies, and ensuring the integrity of the software.

ISO/IEC 23894:2023 offers guidance on risk management for AI technologies. It outlines a structured approach to identifying, assessing, and mitigating risks associated with AI applications. This standard is relevant for organizations seeking to integrate AI into their operations while maintaining a high level of safety and compliance with international standards.

ETSI GR SAI-007:2023 The document is one of the very few that identifies its target audience as designers and implementers who are making assurances to a layperson. The document identifies steps to be taken by AI platform designers and implementers to assure the explicability and transparency of AI processing, which includes AI decision-making and AI data processing.

IEEE P7001:2022 addresses transparency in all autonomous systems, focusing on those capable of causing harm. It includes both physical systems (e.g. automated vehicles) and non-physical systems (e.g. chatbots) and covers machine learning systems and their training datasets. The standard provides a framework for designing and reviewing transparency features, setting requirements, and methods for demonstrating conformance. Future standards may develop from this guideline to focus on specific domains.

NIST AI 100-1:2023 Framework (STD44), developed by the National Institute of Standards and Technology (NIST), provides a comprehensive approach to AI risk management. It emphasizes the need for a thorough understanding of the AI system's behaviour, rigorous testing, and validation to ensure safety. The framework also addresses ethical considerations, such as privacy and non-discrimination, which are increasingly relevant in AI applications. The document includes an Annex B describing how AI risks differ from traditional software risks.

Agile Adaptation
The development of AI systems fits very well with an agile and DevOps approach. If you already have an agile and DevOps approach, it is far easier to establish AI-important processes, such as training, frequent releases, and scaling. See also SafeScrum and DevOps in Chap. 10.

Safety Plan Issues
This depends strongly on the project, context, and the domain in question. We are entering new territory here, especially with high risk AI systems. It is crucial to have clear and detailed steps to ensure these systems are implemented safely and effectively. This includes defining specific procedures, safety protocols, and continuous monitoring to manage any potential risks. Therefore, ensuring that one has familiarity with the relevant standards and guidelines is a good start together with establishing a team of both safety and AI experts.

6.2   Explainable AI (XAI)

Objective
This chapter introduces how explainability of AI systems should be considered when developing AI technologies for the safety-critical domain, keeping in mind that this topic is under rapid development.

Information
This chapter has a direct link to the safety case part AI Safety Report (ASR) encompassing a subpart with the same title.

Explainable AI (XAI) is a research field receiving an increased interest in the last decade (Arrieta et al., 2020). However, both research literature and standards terms such as transparency, interpretability, and explainability are seemingly used interchangeably, challenging a common understanding of XAI (Vatn & Mikalef, 2024).

Explainability of AI Systems from a Technical Perspective
From a technical perspective, XAI might be considered a field concerned with creating "a suite of techniques that produce more explainable models whilst maintaining high performance levels" (Adadi & Berrada, 2018, p. 52138). These techniques are in many instances understood as something that is added on top of AI models that appear as black boxes to extract information about the inner workings of the model. However, explainable models could also be interpretable by design, meaning that the models are explainable without the need of external techniques (Arrieta et al., 2020). The models that need external XAI techniques to be explained could either use model-specific or model-agnostic techniques. The model-agnostic principle could be used for any AI model with the intention to extract some information about the inner workings of the AI model, while the model-specific techniques are only to be used for specific AI models (e.g. deep learning models). The different types of XAI techniques provide different types of explanations, separating between global and local explanations. While the global explanations seek to give an understanding of the overall prediction process of a model, the local explanations focus on explanations in response to a specific input. When developing AI systems, XAI techniques serves as important tools in the development process.

Explainability of AI Systems Considering Human and Organizational Aspects
Recent definitions place the audience as a key aspect when defining XAI (Arrieta et al., 2020; Adadi & Berrada, 2018; Vatn & Mikalef, 2024), underscoring the importance of considering XAI as a multidisciplinary field, which in addition to representing a suite of techniques also considers the recipients of the explanations of the AI systems. By adding both a human and organizational perspective to XAI, one is better equipped to understand how AI systems should be developed and explained to ensure alignment with knowledge on how the human brain processes information. During the design of high risk system, carefully considering this aspect is important to ensure that human operators can serve the controllability function and to avoid confusion and "out of the loop" problems (see Chap. 16). Also, considering organizational aspects is important when developing and implementing XAI

techniques in high risk systems. Different stakeholder groups might have different sets of tasks, responsibilities, information needs, and decision areas attached to their role, and a careful analysis of this when implementing XAI will be important to ensure that people receive the necessary explanations to fulfil their role.

Requirements
The AI Act does not directly address XAI itself (Panigutti et al., 2023). However, the term transparency is given attention (article 13), as well as the principle human oversight (Article 14). Transparency of AI could be described as the opposite of opacity of AI, and in the context of the AI Act it is framed as a tool providing insight into the opacity of AI systems appearing as black boxes (Panigutti et al., 2023). High risk systems shall according to the AI Act—Article 13 be designed to be transparent so deployers can both interpret a system's output and use it appropriately. Article 13 also underscores that high risk AI systems shall have instructions for their use and lists what the instructions should contain as a minimum. There are several requirements, but it is possible to extract several dimensions relating both to the technical aspect of transparency and to the human aspect. For instance, the instruction for use shall include information about technical capabilities and characteristics of the high risk AI system relevant to explain its output. But also, information about the system's performance regarding specific persons or groups of persons on which the system is intended to be used shall be provided. This illustrates that in the context of high risk systems, transparency relates to explainability, as well as the human aspect.

ISO 5469:2024 "AI and functional safety" points at the degree of explainability as an important consideration when assessing risk factors of AI systems and distinguishes between transparency and explainability. While explainability is defined as "the property of an AI system to express important factors influencing the results of the AI system in a way that is understandable to humans" (p. 15), transparency is defined as "the property of a system that appropriate information about the internal processes of an AI system is made available to relevant stakeholders" (p. 15). For system developers, important considerations will be to find the sufficient degree of transparency and explainability. Important questions for developers of high risk AI systems will relate to whether sufficient information about the system is available, how this information should be conveyed to a given recipient, and whether it produces complete and correct results that are reproducible. ISO 5469:2024 also points at explainability approaches that can be used to provide interpretability or explainability into the model structure that might prove helpful in verification and audit processes.

ISO IEC 23984:2023 "AI and risk" underscores how inclusion of stakeholders in development of AI system can help to identify the goals and describe means for enhancing transparency and explainability of AI systems. Lack of both transparency and explainability is listed as a source of risk; however, excessive transparency and explainability are also mentioned to be a potential source of risk relating to confidentiality, intellectual property, and security.

ISO IEC TS 8200:2024 "Controllability" is a relevant standard to consider in relation to explainability of AI systems. Controllability is important to accommodate the principle of human oversight in the AI Act. While degree of explainability might be considered important for a system's controllability, ISO IEC TS 8200: 2024 also points at how controllability might enhance the trust in an AI system that is not fully explainable.

DNV has published a recommended practice DNV RP 0671 "Assurance of AI-enabled systems", which underscores the requirement for evaluating the explainability during the assurance of the trustworthiness of an AI system. The RP also distinguishes between interpretable models that can be understood through its design and models that need additional techniques to be explainable.

Agile Adaptation

The development of AI systems accommodating the requirements for transparency and explainability fits very well with an agile DevOps approach. Considering the evident user aspect in those cases a human is supposed to serve as the controllability function of an AI system, user-centred design principles used in combination with a DevOps approach would be very useful (see Chap. 16).

Safety Plan Issues

When developing high risk AI systems, it is important to have the right balance between transparency, explainability, and maintaining system confidentiality. Different stakeholders, such as manufacturers and users, will require varying levels of detail, so a clear strategy for how and when to communicate these aspects is important. Careful consideration must also be given to ensure that explainability supports the human oversight function without causing confusion or leading to "out of the loop" issues. Regularly updating XAI techniques and refining their alignment with stakeholder needs should be part of the agile DevOps process.

6.3 Safety Of The Intended Functionality (SOTIF)

Objective

The main objective of the SOTIF plan is to describe the planning activities and their justifications to ensure that the risk level associated with hazards related to intended use is taken care of, i.e. are sufficiently low. Related to this, it is important to consider three categories of data—testing data, verification data, and training data.

Acceptance criteria and validation targets are critical for SOTIF safety. Acceptance criteria specify acceptable levels of harm, and validation targets measure efforts to meet these criteria. These should consider relevant operational design domains. Note that UL 4600 lists SOTIF as one of 16 highly recommended hazard identification techniques.

Information

Generally, verification testing helps to ensure the software meets the specified requirements and standards. In contrast, validation testing ensures that the software meets the needs and expectations of the end users (Tank, 2023). See also Chap. 9

about testing in this book. In addition, when dealing with AI systems, we have to consider the training data which are used to "teach" the AI system how to respond to each input and system state. Acceptance criteria, based on verification testing and validation targets, are the most important information used to assure the safety of the intended function (SOTIF) of a system. Acceptance criteria are often defined as an acceptable number of fatalities, injuries, or property damage events in a certain number of hours of operation. Validation target, on the other hand, is the amount of effort required in terms of hours of operation to show that the acceptance criteria are met. See also Chap. 8: "Planning the safety activities: tests, analysis, scenarios, verifications, validations, and regression". It is our experience that descriptions of acceptance criteria and validation targets often overlook factors such as operational design domain (ODD) and operational lifetime.

When it comes to hazards, ISO 21448 defines four sets of scenarios (see also Chap. 9), which are elaborated in the standard:

- Known, not hazardous scenarios
- Known, hazardous scenarios
- Unknown hazardous scenarios
- Unknown, not hazardous scenarios

The safety case arguments must include arguments that all of the four categories of hazardous scenarios mentioned above are handled in a safe way. The SOTIF standard ISO 21448:2022 describes how it could be done.

The safety case needs to handle information related to training data, validations data, and testing data. An important part of the safety case is arguments that the validation data and testing data mirror the needs and requirements of the system's users. For an AI system we also need arguments that the training date is appropriate.

Requirements

As mentioned earlier, we need links between the software product and the test data, validation data, AI training data, and the ODD description. Changes to one of the datasets must be reflected in the other datasets. This will require a large set of links of type "this part of the validation data is dependent on this part of the ODD". In addition to maintenance of the datasets, we will also have the need to maintain all relevant document links.

Agile Adaptation

Changes can and will occur in any software development project. What is special for an agile project is that we claim to embrace changes, also in the ODD. For a SOTIF analysis, this poses an extra challenge since changes to the system's functionality will require extra safety analysis. In addition, it might invalidate some of the current ones.

As a consequence of this, we need a project culture and way of working that always is able to handle changes to the environment and requirements in an efficient manner. If we do this, we are able to start early in the project with a rather imprecise definition of the ODD and the intended functionality. We will then be able to adapt as our ODD understanding increases without introducing errors due to outdated information or misunderstandings.

Safety Plan Issues

Planning for change implies that we document all relevant links/references between all relevant documents—especially links between:

- ODD, test data, validation data, and training data
- Requirements, test data, and validation data
- ODD, requirements, and software product

As we learn more about the ODD—users, the operating environment, and so on—the amount of unknown scenarios, hazardous or not—will shrink. This will improve the possibilities for relevant safety analysis and thus increase our confidence in the analysis of the safety of the intended functionality of the system.

Chapter 7
Stakeholders and Organizations

This chapter addresses stakeholders and organizations by first outlining different stakeholder groups to consider in the context of high risk AI systems. Next, it discusses relevant organizational aspects and underscores the importance of safety culture.

7.1 Stakeholders

Objective
This chapter describes how stakeholders should be considered when developing high risk AI systems in accordance with the AI Act. It builds on the traditional roles within development projects within safety organizations and considers the new roles AI brings into these development projects.

Information
Stakeholder considerations are important in the development, design, and assurance of high risk AI systems. Stakeholders might be considered through two angles in the context of the AI Act. The *first* angle relates to formal responsibilities relating to where in the value chain of the high risk AI system you reside, specifically underscored by Sect. 3 in Chap. 3 in the AI Act outlining the obligations of "providers" and "deployers" of high risk AI systems and other parties, as well as Sect. 4 in Chap. 3 addressing notifying authorities and notified bodies. The AI Act defines eight stakeholders; deployer, authorized representative, importer, distributor, operator, notifying authority, conformity assessment body, and notified body. The *second* angle relates to the principle of human oversight (Article 14) that, in many instances, will require a careful stakeholder focus on the system design process (Fig. 7.1).

AI-Specific Roles
While the development of high risk AI systems makes it relevant to consider the traditional roles of safety organizations, ISO/IEC 22989:2022—Artificial

© The Author(s) 2025
T. Myklebust et al., *The AI Act and The Agile Safety Plan*, SpringerBriefs in Computer Science, https://doi.org/10.1007/978-3-031-80504-2_7

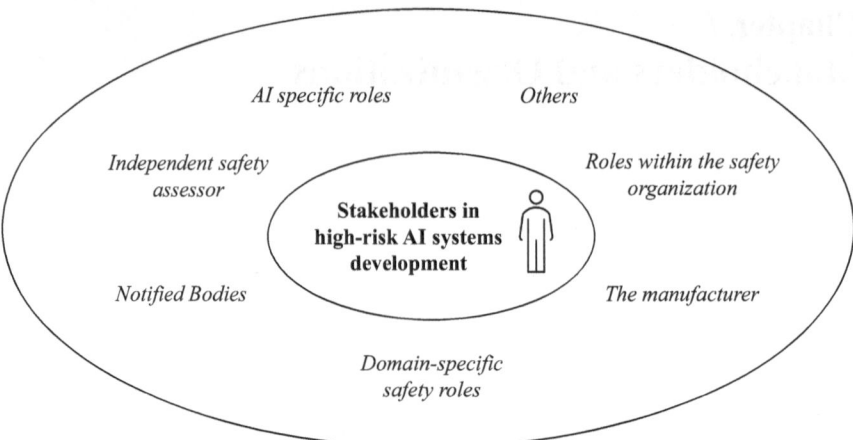

Fig. 7.1 Stakeholders in high risk AI systems development

Intelligence concepts and terminology—points at specific roles that applies in the context of AI. This standard provides an overview of different AI stakeholder roles relating to the AI provider, AI producer, AI customer, AI partner, AI subject, and authorities (policymakers and regulators). Safety organizations should carefully reflect on how the development of high risk AI systems brings in new roles in the development projects, and how this changes the overall work processes and organization. The deployer is not described in this standard, but Sect. 6.2.5 includes information regarding deployment.

Stakeholders in the Context of a Development Project Within a Safety Organization

In a typical development project of a safety organization, there are both internal and external roles that are relevant to be aware of. Internally in agile projects, you often have a project manager, a scrum master with a scrum team, RAMS responsible, and a safety plan and safety case author. Externally, these would need to deal with assessors, validators, and independent testers at some point in the development project. The degree to which the tester and validator need to be independent depends on the SILx.

The Manufacturer

The Blue Guide (EA, 2022) outlines the manufacturer's responsibilities under Union harmonization legislation in Sect. 3.1 (pp. 34–38). A summary is presented here: A manufacturer is any person who designs or has a product manufactured and places it on the market under their name or trademark. They must ensure the product complies with legal requirements, including performing conformity assessments and maintaining traceability. They are also required to cooperate with authorities if a product poses risks or is non-compliant. Manufacturers retain full responsibility for compliance, even when outsourcing production. They must provide documentation, such as technical files and certificates, to demonstrate compliance. If a product is altered or modified, the party making changes assumes the manufacturer's role.

Domain-Specific Safety Roles

While several roles of a development project in a safety organization (e.g. project manager, safety case author) are similar across domains, there will also be instances where specific high risk domains have their specific roles. For instance, within railways, the EU legislation CENECEL EN 5012X standards and IEC safety standards provide an overview and description of the main railway and safety roles. On the other hand, within automotive, the ISO 26262 series describes the roles in a more generic approach, e.g. describing "Roles and responsibilities in safety management" in ISO 26262-2:2010. A stakeholder analysis in the context of high risk AI systems would therefore need to carefully address the specific domain the system is developed for to ensure that the relevant stakeholder in each case is considered.

Notified Bodies (NoBo)

The EU has established a system for the notification of notified bodies. In the EU, notification is an act whereby a Member State in the EU or the EEA informs the Commission and the other Member States that a body that fulfils the relevant requirements has been designated to carry out conformity assessment according to a regulation or directive. Notification of notified bodies and their withdrawal are the responsibility of the notifying Member State. The list of notified bodies can be found at the official website of the European Union (EU, 2024b). Notified bodies often also perform independent assessments, as the work of the independent safety assessor (ISA) and NoBo is closely linked.

Independent Safety Assessor

The independent safety assessor or independent assessor team is an independent person or often a certification body appointed to carry out the safety assessment. Confined to safety, independent safety assessment evaluates a system with respect to safety and its operation and use. The safety assessment may, for example, be performed on the basis of a safety case.

Other Stakeholders Beyond the Typical Development Project

In addition to the internal and external stakeholders within the safety organization relating to the specific development projects, it is also relevant to consider additional stakeholders in the context of high risk AI systems. Several high risk AI systems might in the future be used to transport people. Carefully addressing passengers as a stakeholder group will be important. For instance, research points at gender differences in the safety experience of men and women taking autonomous buses (Myklebust et al., 2021).

Requirements

Chapter 3 on high risk systems in the AI Act provides in Sect. 3 an outlining of the obligations of providers and deployers of these systems. As a provider, article 16 outlines that companies providing high risk AI systems need to meet specific standards and mark their product with CE marking. In those cases that harmonized standards are not developed yet, the AI Act outlines how the providers must ensure that their systems undergo a specific assessment procedure in article 43. This can also be seen in connection with article 21 outlining how providers of high risk AI systems must cooperate with competent authorities. While the AI Act points at several obligations of providers, also importers and distributors are mentioned, in addition to a separate section (Sect. 4) on notifying bodies and notified bodies. According to article 23 "Obligation of Importers", importers are responsible ensuring that high risk AI systems they sell meets all regulatory requirements, including checking the assessment procedure of the product, documentation, and its CE marking. Importers are also required to store certificates and instructions for 10 years and cooperate with relevant authorities. Also, distributors have specific obligations in the AI Act, outlined in article 24. While there are specific articles addressing obligations for importers (article 23) and distributors (article 24), article 25 outlines the responsibilities along the AI value chain. It states that "any distributor, importer, deployer or other third party shall be considered to be a provider of a high-risk system" under certain circumstances. For instance, this applies if they put their trademark on the system, make changes to the system, or modify its intended purpose.

DNV RP-0671 underscores that stakeholder focus is a part of the assurance process of AI-enabled systems, and this focus should be kept throughout the lifecycle of an AI-enabled system. Stakeholder considerations should be brought in by identifying who they are in the context of a given high risk AI system, analysing needs, and capturing how these needs might direct the assurance effort.

Also, ISO 5469 "Artificial intelligence—Functional safety and AI system" implicitly brings in the importance of stakeholders in relation to the explainability of AI systems, pointing out that explainability evaluations should be regarded as part of the general evaluation of an AI system, and whether the output is understandable will often depend on who the recipient is (e.g. system developer, first responders, and bystanders).

Agile Adaptations

DNV RP-0671 underscores that stakeholder interests are revisited and updated, underscoring the importance of an agile approach that considers stakeholder interests. Also, there might be conflicting interests—assurance might serve as a basis for agreeing on trade-offs. The fact that the explainability of an AI system is highly audience-dependent also points to the importance of an agile stakeholder focus, ensuring that design processes seek to accommodate human oversight.

Safety Plan Issues

Early in the project, evaluate the relevant stakeholders. This includes stakeholders across the value chain, such as providers, deployers, and authorities, and underscores the importance of human oversight in the design process. Especially, one should consider new roles that AI introduces into traditional safety organizations and the importance of addressing domain-specific roles in high risk sectors.

7.2 Safety Organization

Objective

This part of the agile safety plan should describe relevant safety organizations for the manufacturers, ensuring competence, experience, independence, training, and communication.

Information

Safety organization is an important part of a development project. How it is organized depends on the context, project, and system to be developed. A safety team is crucial for the development, deployment, and operation of safety-critical systems. This team identifies potential risks, develops mitigation strategies, and ensures compliance with safety standards and regulations.

This part is linked to the "Organizational structure" chapter of the QMR and the "Safety organization" chapter of the SMR and to the "Organizational structure" chapter of the QMR and the "Safety organization" chapter of the SMR.

Requirements

The AI Act does not include concrete requirements for a safety organization, but risk management is an important part of it. For further information, see Chap. 8.

To check how the project should be organized safety-wise, we need answers to one question: Are all planned positions filled with people with the right competence and experience? We might also need to check if the project's organization fulfils relevant standards and independence requirements.

Safety standards outline several key organizational responsibilities for developing safety-critical systems. They emphasize the management of functional safety and stress the importance of training and maintaining appropriate competence levels. Verification and functional safety assessment require proper oversight to ensure these processes are effectively managed.

ISO 26262 series is one of the few safety standards that includes requirements related to distributed teams. Distributed development is defined as *development of an item or element (3.41) with development responsibility divided between the customer and supplier(s) for the entire item or element.*

Requirements for distributed development are presented in ISO 26262-6:2018 Clause E.2.3 "Safety analyses in a distributed software development (including SEooC development of software elements)" and ISO 26262-8:2018 Clause 5 "Interfaces within distributed developments".

For more information, see Chap. 8 and Sect. 19.2.

Agile Adaptations

The agile safety organization should be structured to promote efficiency, clear communication, and quick adaptation to changes. It typically includes key roles such as developers, assessors, safety managers, and independent safety assessors (ISA). These stakeholders collaborate closely throughout the project to ensure that safety is maintained as an integral part of the development process, rather than something added at the end.

The agile safety organization focuses on continuous updates, shortening the time between code completion and safety case finalization and reducing the amount of required documentation. This approach allows the organization to manage changes more effectively during development and after the system's release. The safety team is also responsible for ensuring compliance with standards such as EN 50129 and monitoring system safety throughout its lifecycle, with a strong emphasis on communication and collaboration between all stakeholders.

The chapter "2.6 Alongside Engineering" (Myklebust & Stålhane, 2021) describes how functional safety teams operate when developing a safety-critical system.

Safety Plan Issues
Manufacturers should focus on competence, experience, independence, training, and communication. The plan should highlight the importance of organizing a safety team based on the project's context, ensuring that safety-critical systems are developed, deployed, and operated effectively. The plan should ensure that it is assessed whether all necessary positions are filled with competent individuals and if the project complies with relevant standards, including, if relevant, ISO 26262 requirements for distributed teams. Agile adaptations emphasize efficient communication, quick responses to changes, and continuous updates, reducing documentation while ensuring compliance with safety standards.

7.3   Safety Culture

Objective
This chapter outlines how safety culture is an organizational aspect that is highly relevant to consider in the context of high risk AI systems development and provides references to standards elaborating on the topic.

Information
This chapter of the safety plan links to the Quality Management Report (QMR) in the safety case.

Safety Culture as Organizational Culture
The concept of "culture" is originally an anthropological concept brought into the corporate environment to describe patterns in artefacts and behaviours, serving several functions that ultimately should contribute to the success of organizations (Furnham, 2005). This is facilitated by contributing to representing social glue, as well as by creating a shared system of meaning useful for mutual understanding. Within the safety-critical domain, culture is considered essential to guide human and organizational behaviour in a manner that might reduce the risk for mishaps (Lee et al. 2017). Focusing on organizational culture by working with policies, structures, and other organizational issues, companies might directly affect their safety outcomes. This might in many instances be regarded as more effective to

increase overall safety outcomes than focusing narrowly on changing individuals' attitudes, beliefs, and values (Lee et al., 2017).

Safety Culture in Safety Standards

ISO 26262-1:2018—Road Vehicles—Functional Safety defines safety culture as *"enduring values, attitudes, motivations and knowledge of an organization in which safety is prioritized over competing gals in decisions and behaviour"* (p. 22). Also, ISO 26262-2:2018 of this standard underscores that safety organizations should pay attention to how safety culture can be developed and sustained, being an important facilitator of the effective achievement of functional safety. Safety culture can be understood as consisting of two important aspects relating to both personal dedication and integrity of different people important to the safety activities within the organization, as well as the overall "safety thinking" that is part of the organization. This "safety thinking" might be visible in that individuals are feel safe to ask questions, commit to excellence, and feel safe to admit mistakes when they occur. Part 2 of ISO 26262-8:2018 Annex B provides also a concrete table with examples serving as indications of both poor safety culture and a good safety culture (p. 33).

EN 50129 specifically underscores that safety management processes should be implemented under the control of an appropriate safety organization, assigning roles to people with competency to fill them. While safety culture is not specifically addressed, most organizational researchers would acknowledge that culture is a major aspect when addressing organizational issues. In the Safety-Critical Systems Club (SCSC) Data guide 2024, organizational culture is considered an important aspect of establishing context and understanding a specific organization. In an appendix a short questionnaire on Data Safety Culture is provided, serving as a practical tool measuring individual's views on safety risks relating to data.

Requirements

The EU AI Act has indirect requirements related to safety culture, particularly for high risk AI systems. It mandates risk management systems, human oversight, and post-market monitoring to ensure safety and prevent harm throughout the AI system's lifecycle.

Within the railway domain, safety culture was included in the EU railway law (2016/798, art. 29). However, it is worth noting that safety culture within that context to a large extent points at safety culture as part of the internal safety organizations, more than it being a concept addressing the whole ecosystem within railway.

While several safety standards underscore the importance of safety culture, it might be challenging to extract clear requirements. ISO 26262-2 and ISO 26262-8 include safety culture requirements. ISO 26262-2 also includes an informative Annex B regarding safety culture. Also, UL4600:2023 provides a chapter on the topic, and SCSC Data guide 2024 connects the concept of safety culture to data safety specifically.

Agile Adaptation

Safety culture should be considered an organizational issue that needs to be worked on continuously. This underscores the usefulness of an "agile approach" to understanding how safety culture is developed, updated, and maintained within safety organizations.

Safety Plan Issues

The safety plan should address key issues related to safety culture, emphasizing its role in guiding human and organizational behaviour to reduce risks. Safety culture, as defined by standards like ISO 26262, focuses on the values, attitudes, and behaviours that prioritize safety over competing goals. It also highlights the importance of personal dedication, integrity, and an organizational "safety mindset", where individuals feel safe to ask questions and admit mistakes. Developing and maintaining a safety culture requires continuous organizational effort, often benefiting from an agile approach to ensure it evolves with safety needs.

Chapter 8
Compliance with Regulations, AI, and Functional Safety Standards

This chapter addresses the crucial aspect of ensuring compliance with AI and functional safety standards, focusing on adherence to the EU AI Act and related regulations. It highlights the importance of maintaining a risk-based approach to classify AI systems according to their risk levels. The stringent requirements for high risk AI systems are underscored, including conformity assessments and CE marking. We also discuss the need for continuous adaptation and flexibility in regulatory compliance to keep pace with evolving standards and technological advancements.

Objective

This part of the safety plan's objective is to ensure that the EU AI Act and safety regulations and other identified regulations are adhered to in a safe, reliable, and trustworthy manner. This includes the development, deployment, and utilization of artificial intelligence (AI) systems. It also includes adhering to a risk-based regulatory framework that categorizes AI systems by unacceptable, high, limited, and minimal risk levels to implement necessary safeguards, ensure transparency, and mitigate risks associated with AI technologies.

Information

The high risk AI systems are subject to strict regulatory requirements to ensure they do not pose undue risks to individuals or society. Compliance with these regulations involves rigorous conformity assessments, including adherence to specific standards and obtaining CE marking, which is mandatory for placing these systems on the EU market. The CE marking serves as a declaration by the manufacturer that the product meets all applicable EU safety, health, and environmental protection requirements. This includes meeting the essential requirements set out in the AI Act for AI systems classified as high risk systems. The conformity assessment process for CE marking typically involves third-party evaluations by notified bodies to verify compliance. Once certified, the CE marking must be visibly affixed to the product, signalling its conformity to EU standards and enabling its free circulation within the European Economic Area (EEA).

T. Myklebust et al., *The AI Act and The Agile Safety Plan*, SpringerBriefs in Computer Science, https://doi.org/10.1007/978-3-031-80504-2_8

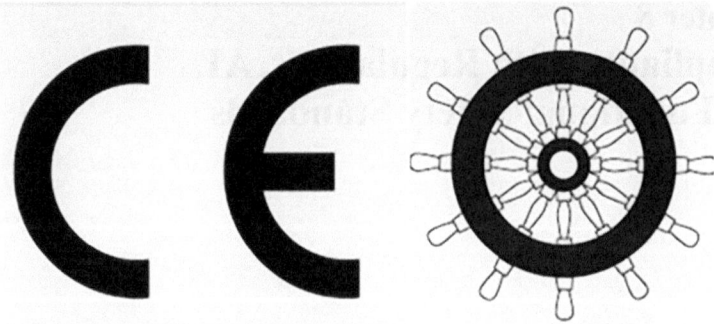

Fig. 8.1 The CE and wheel marks

Some of the relevant regulations and directives that require a CE mark and are relevant for safe AI systems:

- Electromagnetic Compatibility (EMC) Directive 2014/30/EU
- Radio Equipment Directive (RED) 2014/53/EU
- Construction Products Regulation (CPR) 305/2011
- Equipment for potentially explosive atmospheres (ATEX) Directive 2014/34/EU

According to the Directive 2014/90/EU (Marine equipment), maritime products require the wheel mark (Fig. 8.1).

Requirements

The AI Act (Regulation (EU) 2024/1689) contains several important articles and annexes specifically focused on high risk AI systems. These requirements establish the framework for classifying, regulating, and ensuring compliance for AI systems that are considered high risk due to their potential impact on fundamental rights, health, safety, or the environment. Table 8.1 summarizes the main articles and annexes related to high risk AI systems and examples of relevant standards and guidelines. Requirements related to providers and importers are not included.

Table 8.1 The main AI articles and relevant standards and guidelines

AI Act's main articles related to SW development of high risk systems	Examples of relevant standards and guidelines Some of the standards are commented in Chap. 6
Article 6 Classification rules for high risk AI systems	There are no standards that classify high risk AI systems. Safety standards classify, for example, different SILx levels. The ISO/IEC 5469:2024 (STD33) classifies different AI Technology Classes, including different usage levels. Usage level Ax is AI technology used in a safety-related system. Usage level Bx is AI technology used during development, and usage level C is AI technology used to assist safety functions. Usage Level D is assigned if the AI technology is not part of a safety function in the E/E/PE
Article 7 Amendments to Annex III	See comments to Annex III below

(continued)

Table 8.1 (continued)

AI Act's main articles related to SW development of high risk systems	Examples of relevant standards and guidelines Some of the standards are commented in Chap. 6
Article 8 Compliance with the requirements	Concretized in FuSa and AI standards but they are not sufficient today. So, other concretizations have to be included. And risk mitigation achieved by existing standards? Probably not. Relevant standards that combine FuSa and AI are only: • CEN/CLC/TR 17894 Artificial Intelligence Conformity Assessment (STD52) • ISO IEC 5469:2024 (STD33); see also Sect. 1.2 • DNV-RP-0671:2023 (STD8) Assurance of AI-enabled systems. See also Chap. 5
Article 9 Risk management systems	The basic or umbrella IEC 61508 standard and related safety standards • ISO/IEC 42001:2023 Information technology—Artificial intelligence—Management system (STD31) • ISO/IEC 23894:2023 Information technology—Artificial intelligence—Guidance on risk management (STD35) • NIST AI 100–1:2023 Framework: Artificial Intelligence Risk Management (STD44) • ISO 31000:2018 Risk management—Guidelines (STD28) • IEC 31010:2019 Risk management—Risk assessment techniques (STD13)
Article 10 Data and data governance	• Data safety guidance 127 (STD6) • ISO 8000 data quality series (STD39)
Article 11 Technical documentation	See Annex IV below
Article 12 Record-keeping	• ISO 9001 (STD23)
Article 14 Human oversight	The report (National Transportation Safety Board [NTSB], 2019) includes a presentation of regulatory gaps, and it seems that there generally seems to be a lack of standards specifically addressing this topic Myklebust et al. (2025) Chap. 16
Article 15 Accuracy, robustness, and cybersecurity	• BIPM on uncertainty (STD1) • DIN on uncertainty (STD7) • DNV-RP-06712023 (STD8) includes uncertainty, aleatory and epistemic • ISO/IEC TS 22440 (STD34) includes robustness requirements • ISO/IEC 21448:2022 (STD27) includes robustness requirements • IEC 62443 cybersecurity series (STD19) • ISO/SAE 21434 on cybersecurity (STD40) • Radio Equipment Directive (RED) 2014/53/EU (Reg. 2) • EN 18031 series (STD58). Harmonized standards for RED • SAE J3101 (STD48) on HW-protected security • Kiureghian et al. (2009) on Aleatory or epistemic?
Article 17 Quality management	• ISO 9001 (STD23) • EN 50129 (STD11) • *The Agile Safety Case* (Myklebust & Stålhane, 2018). QMR part • Myklebust et al. (2025). QMR part

(continued)

Table 8.1 (continued)

AI Act's main articles related to SW development of high risk systems	Examples of relevant standards and guidelines Some of the standards are commented in Chap. 6
Article 18 Documentation keeping	• ISO 9001 (STD23)
Article 21 Cooperation with competent authorities	According to the AI Act, each EU Member States should designate a national supervisory authority to supervise the application and implementation of the AI Act. • Blue guide (EA, 2022) • EU AI office (EU, 2024a). The European AI Office is the centre of AI expertise across the EU • Notified bodies (EU, 2024b) • NB-Rail [NB-Rail] • Railway InterOperability Directive (IOD) 2016/797 (REG. 16)
Article 26 Obligations of deployers of high risk AI systems	• Some safety standards like EN 50716:2023 (STD12) include requirements for deployment • Standards like ISO 24089:2023 (STD24) on SW update • UL 5500:2018 (STD51) on remote SW update • ITU Telecommunication and X.1373:2017 STD41 include requirements for SW updates over the air
Article 40 Harmonized standards	See Sect. 1.3. And AI Act Article 43, "Conformity assessment", which includes relevant information regarding harmonized standards, especially when they are unavailable or include limitations. • Blue guide (EA, 2022) • EU link regarding harmonized standards (EU, 2024c) • The EN 50126–2:2017 (STD9) standard was recognized as a harmonized standard in the EU Official Journal (European Commission, 2020). See "fun facts" in the box below
Article 60 Testing of high risk AI systems in real-world conditions outside AI regulatory sandboxes	See Chap. 9
Annex III—High risk AI systems	In this book, we focus on high risk AI systems for the process industry, automotive, railway, and seaborne
Annex IV—Technical documentation	• EN 50129 (STD11) • The Agile Safety Case book (Myklebust & Stålhane, 2018) • Myklebust et al. (2014) • Proof of Compliance book (Myklebust & Stålhane, 2021) • Annex A of this book • ISO/IEC 5469:2024 (STD33) • UNECE Regulation 156 (REG. 30) • ISO/SAE 21434 (STD44) • IEC 62443 series (STD19) • EU declaration of conformity (EU, 2024d)
Annexes VI-VII— Conformity assessment procedures	• EU conformity assessment (EU, 2024e) • CEN/CLC/TR 17894 Artificial Intelligence Conformity (STD52)

Here is a fun fact regarding harmonized standards. An example
The railway domain has long experience using harmonized standards. The EN 50126–2:2017 (STD9) for railway has been issued, including Annex ZZ *"(informative) Relationship between this European Standard and the Essential Requirements of EU Directive 2008/57/EC"* in 2017. The standards state, *"2018-07-03 is the latest date by which this document has to be implemented at the national level" and that 2020-07-03 is the latest date by which the national standards conflicting with this document have to be withdrawn"*.

Copy from the Official Journal (European Commission, 2020): "Article 1 The references of harmonized standards drafted in support of Directive 2008/57/EC, listed in Annex I to this Decision, are hereby published in the Official Journal of the European Union". EN 50126–2:2017 is listed in Annex I.

Agile Adaptation
An agile mindset is crucial in the rapidly evolving landscape of AI and functional safety regulations and requirements. Agile adaptation involves maintaining flexibility in processes and planning to respond quickly to changes in regulations, harmonized standards, and technological advancements. All organizations should foster a culture that encourages iterative development and continuous learning to ensure compliance while staying ahead of new regulatory demands.

Safety Plan Issues
It is important to continuously monitor the regulatory environment and the development of new standards and update of existing standards. A flexible and dynamic planning approach is necessary to integrate updates and changes into compliance strategies. This ensures that the organization promptly addresses emerging risks and aligns with the latest regulatory requirements.

Chapter 9
Planning Tests, Analysis, Scenarios, Verification, Validation, and Regression

This chapter focuses on planning tests, analysis, scenarios, verification, validation, and regression testing to ensure the reliability and safety of systems. It outlines the importance of systematic test methodologies, including scenario-based evaluations and simulations, to verify compliance with safety requirements and validate system performance. The chapter emphasizes the role of regression testing in maintaining system integrity after updates, highlighting how agile practices and automated tools can facilitate frequent testing and quicker resolution of potential issues. These methods ensure systems meet safety standards and operate reliably in real-world conditions.

Objective
The objective of this chapter is to show how to plan for test methodologies and procedures for systematically assessing, confirming, and maintaining the reliability and effectiveness of safety measures. This includes rigorous testing, thorough analysis, scenario evaluation, simulations, compliance verification, system validation, and regression testing to ensure that it is a safe system.

Information
When developing safety-critical software, rigorous testing, verification, validation, analysis, and regression testing are essential to ensure its reliability and safety in all scenarios. Scenarios have to be closely developed as part of the DoS, ODD, and ConOps in Chap. 3.

The functional safety standards do not emphasize the scenario approach, but this will be improved in the future. A scenario approach involves testing safety-critical systems in real-world situations, including edge and corner cases. For an AV, this could, for instance, be unexpected conditions, such as heavy snow or low sunlight, to ensure the system's reliability and safety under relevant circumstances. In trial operations and demonstrations, Acted-out scenarios, also known as Role-played scenarios, are common. This involves testing scenarios based on real-world human behaviour, often mimicking how people or systems might behave under various conditions.

T. Myklebust et al., *The AI Act and The Agile Safety Plan*, SpringerBriefs in
Computer Science, https://doi.org/10.1007/978-3-031-80504-2_9

Current standards like IEC 61508, ISO 26262, and EN 50716:2023 do not include scenario definitions as a required activity. The EU automotive regulation 2022/1426 (REG. 31) for Automatic Driving Systems (ADS) includes three relevant scenario definitions:

- *19 'nominal traffic scenarios' means reasonably foreseeable situations encountered by the ADS when operating within its ODD. These scenarios represent the non-critical interactions of the ADS with other traffic participants and generate normal operation of the ADS.*
- *20. 'critical scenarios' means scenarios related to edge-cases (e.g. unexpected conditions with an exceptionally low probability of occurrence) and operational insufficiencies, not limited to traffic conditions but also including environmental conditions (e.g. heavy rain or low sunlight glaring cameras), human factors, connectivity and miscommunication leading to emergency operation of the ADS.*
- *21. 'failure scenarios' means the scenarios related to ADS and/or vehicle components failure which may lead to normal or emergency operation of the ADS depending on whether or not the minimum safety level is preserved.*

ISO 21448 was developed and issued in 2022 to address some important parts that had not been sufficiently included in the ISO 26262 series (see Sect. 6.3).

The standards below cover several aspects when developing, testing, and validating ADS that could be also considered for other system types.

- ISO 34501:2022 (STD53)—Defines the terms and concepts used in test scenarios for ADS, primarily applicable to Level 3 and above systems. This standard ensures that a common language is used across the industry, facilitating better communication and understanding.

  - This standard includes a slightly different definition of scenario than the 2022/1426 regulation (REG. 31): "*3.4 scenario sequence of scenes (3.6) usually including the ADS/subject vehicle(s), and its/their interactions in the process of performing the dynamic driving task (DDT)*".

- ISO 34502:2022 (STD54)—Provides a framework for scenario-based safety evaluation during the development of ADS. It guides the safety evaluation process to ensure that the ADS performs reliably within its designated operational design domain (ODD).
- ISO 34503:2023 (STD55)—Focuses on the specification of the ODD, detailing the conditions under which an ADS is designed to operate. This standard is essential for defining the capabilities and limitations of ADS, which is critical for both developers and regulators.
- ISO 34504:2024 (STD56)—Proposes a method for categorizing test scenarios, aiming to harmonize the classification across different databases and studies. This categorization is vital for consistent and comprehensive scenario coverage during testing.
- ISO 34505: Draft 2024 (STD57)—Provides methodologies for evaluating scenarios and converting them into test cases. It includes criteria for prioritizing and

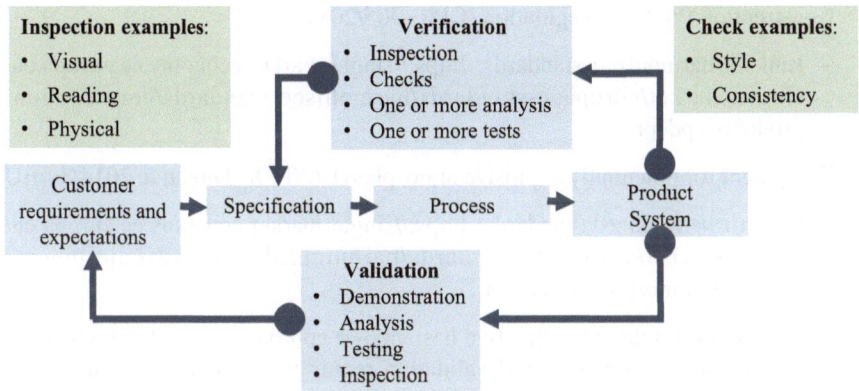

Fig. 9.1 The relationship between verification and validation together with different V&V aspects

optimizing test cases based on factors like frequency and criticality, ensuring comprehensive and efficient testing.

During our projects, we conducted several interviews and discussed verification and validation. International standards define V&V differently, so a clarification is presented in Fig. 9.1.

Regression testing verifies that recent code changes have not introduced new bugs or errors or negatively affected a system's existing functionality. It involves re-running the previously successful tests to ensure the stability and integrity of the software after updates or modifications. This practice is crucial in maintaining the system's overall reliability as it evolves.

This part links to the "V&V" chapter of the Safety Management Report (SMR) part of the safety case (see Chap. 1). This chapter, in the safety case, contains several relevant safety case references. For further information, see Annex A.

Requirements

The AI Act has several requirements related to tests, analysis, scenarios, verification, validation, and regression testing (see Table 8.1). The plan is, in the future, to develop relevant harmonized standards for the AI Act regarding tests, analysis, scenarios, verification, validation, and regression testing.

Other relevant regulations and directives have already issued an overview of relevant harmonized standards:

- Electromagnetic Compatibility (EMC) Directive 2014/30/EU

  - Link to harmonized standards: https://single-market-economy.ec.europa.eu/single-market/european-standards/harmonised-standards/electromagnetic-compatibility-emc_en

- Radio Equipment Directive (RED) 2014/53/EU

  - Link to harmonized standards: https://single-market-economy.ec.europa.eu/single-market/european-standards/harmonised-standards/radio-equipment_en

- Construction Products Regulation (CPR) 305/2011

    - Link to harmonized standards: https://single-market-economy.ec.europa.eu/
      single-market/european-standards/harmonised-standards/construction-
      products-cpdcpr_en

- Equipment for potentially explosive atmospheres (ATEX) Directive 2014/34/EU

    - Link to harmonized standards: https://single-market-economy.ec.europa.eu/
      single-market/european-standards/harmonised-standards/equipment-
      explosive-atmospheres-atex_en

The Maritime Equipment Directive has another approach. A related regulation, providing testing, verification, and validation requirements, is being issued on a yearly basis. The last updated implementing regulation (EU) 2024/1975 (REG. 15) amending the MED in force from 4 September 2024. Link to relevant standards: https://eur-lex.europa.eu/eli/reg_impl/2024/1975/oj

IMO has a Formal Safety Assessment (FSA) approach that emphasizes a scenario approach (IMO FSA 2018). This method assesses risks related to maritime activities and evaluates the costs and benefits of various safety measures. It is a structured, proactive process aimed at enhancing maritime safety through risk analysis and cost-benefit evaluation.

Normative standards: A normative standard is a document to which reference is made in the standard in such a way as to make the application indispensable. It normally contains a clause named "Normative standards". IEC 61508 standards and EN 5012X standards include normative references, for, e.g., environmental requirements, while ISO 26262-X standards only mention the other parts of the standard series in the ISO 26262-X standard.

According to the ERA Guide [ERA/GUI/07-2011/INT] ch.3.2.5: "Where a standard referred to in a Technical Specification for Interoperability (TSI), e.g., Regulation (EU) 2016/919 (REG. 32) contains a reference to another standard unless otherwise provided in the TSI, this second standard also becomes mandatory." The control, command, and signalling TSI are related to the normative references in the mandatory standards. The references are listed in the chapter "Normative references" in these standards.

> It is common to believe, even for safety engineers, that products declared by their manufacturer to conform with the EMC directive must be free from EMC problems. However, the directive is concerned mainly with removing technical barriers to trade.

Agile Adaptation
Regression testing is more important due to more frequent releases. Current safety standards are weak when it comes to regression testing requirements. It is important to be able to repeat tests frequently and without too many additional costs to ensure

that all relevant parts of previously checked code still operate as intended—as defined by tests. Regression testing has three benefits—it creates confidence with developers that the system operates as intended, that recent changes do not make previously checked code fail, and that it is OK to move on. It also creates confidence with other stakeholders, e.g. the customer, that the system performs as intended.

With the recent adaptation of agile methods such as SafeScrum to the development of safety-critical systems and efficient tools for test automation, it is possible to do regression testing of larger parts of the system with increased frequency without adding extra cost. First, practices such as test-first development enable testers to continuously develop the test suite alongside—in parallel with—creating code—reducing the need for dedicated testers. Secondly, by using tools (e.g. testing and analysis tools), testing, and integration frameworks, tests can be repeated more often, e.g., through a nightly build regime. In this way, all potential conflicts or errors caused by recent changes to the codebase will be known shortly after they have been introduced and can thus be resolved when the knowledge about the code is fresh in mind. The problems are thus easier to resolve.

Two of the authors have developed relevant adapted practices and approaches such as:

- The Agile Hazard Log (Myklebust et al., 2017)
- The agile FMEA approach (Myklebust et al., 2018b)
- Agile practices when developing safety systems. (Myklebust et al., 2018a)
- Analyse first development (Myklebust et al., 2019)

Safety Plan Issues

It is important to emphasize rigorous testing and validation processes to ensure the reliability and safety of safety systems. Over time, it has become more important to develop scenario-based safety evaluation. Be aware of agile practices when improving regression testing, as this may enable more frequent and cost-effective testing to maintain system integrity through continuous updates.

Chapter 10
Software and AI Lifecycles

This chapter first provides insights into the different phases of a software lifecycle, describing how DevOps as a methodology might make software development and delivery more efficient. Also, the SafeScrum approach is briefly described. The chapter next focuses on AI lifecycles and provides insight into two approaches to developing safety-critical AI: EASA's W-shaped process model for machine learning (ML) applications and the Safety Assurance of Autonomous Systems in Complex Environments (SACE) process.

10.1 Software Lifecycles

Objective

This section's objective is to provide a defined set of safety and software lifecycle processes for each development phase when developing products/systems. This includes facilitating communication among stakeholders of the lifecycles. An additional objective is to identify activities at each phase throughout the lifecycle to implement a certain level of functional safety.

Introduction

This subchapter has links to similar chapters in the safety case. Safety lifecycle, waterfall models, V-model, and agile methods like SafeScrum are all currently used for software development.

It seems practical to start with IEEE's definition (IEEE, 1990), which defines what is covered by a software lifecycle—safety or not: The software lifecycle typically includes a concept phase, requirements phase, design phase, implementation phase, test phase, installation and checkout phase, operation and maintenance phase, and, sometimes, retirement phase.

T. Myklebust et al., *The AI Act and The Agile Safety Plan*, SpringerBriefs in Computer Science, https://doi.org/10.1007/978-3-031-80504-2_10

Requirements

The EU AI Act does not explicitly use the term "software lifecycle", but it addresses similar concepts, particularly in the context of high risk AI systems. The Act requires continuous risk management throughout the entire lifecycle of these systems, covering everything from design and development to deployment and post-market monitoring. It emphasizes the need for ongoing testing, updates, and compliance checks to ensure that the AI system remains safe and effective as it evolves. Essentially, the Act indirectly ensures that all software lifecycle stages are managed to minimize risks. See also Chaps. 5 and 8.

Software lifecycle processes consist of a chain of dependent activities based on requirements. Note that requirements may come from customers, inside the development organization, the government, or the applicable standards. A useful process description should focus on how, why, and by whom. In addition, it must promote communication among its users.

Each process activity description must contain the following information:

- Why the activity is needed—its purpose
- What input is needed for the activity to fulfil its purpose?
- What are the criteria the input needs to fulfil?
- What output will it generate—why and for which other activities?
- How will the necessary output be generated?
- What are the criteria the output needs to fulfil before the activity can be considered finished—at least temporarily?

All development activities, except the first and the last, must both receive input and generate output to one or more other process activities. A god example of a software safety lifecycle is the one shown in IEC 61508–1, fig. 2. The lifecycle model is generic—i.e. it says what should be done, not how to do it.

Agile Adaptation

Irrespective of development concept, things will change over time—e.g. requirements, environment, or customer needs and expectations. What is special about agile development is that we **embrace change**—we expect it, prepare for it, and handle it in a controlled, safe, and reliable way.

In order to be able to handle changes in a safe and reliable way, we need to know which parts of the development process and finished parts of the system that will be affected by the (proposed) changes. This can be done based on the documentation of the issues listed under "Requirements".

DevOps is a methodology that brings development and operations teams together to make software development and delivery more efficient—see Fig. 10.1. DataOps focuses on breaking down silos between data producers and data consumers to make data more valuable. In the future, we expect that DevOps, DataOps, and, e.g., ML-Ops will also be used when developing safety-critical systems.

SafeScrum is so far (Hanssen et al., 2018) mainly described for the SW development part, i.e. in phase 10 of IEC 61508. Thus, one may, e.g., include other phases

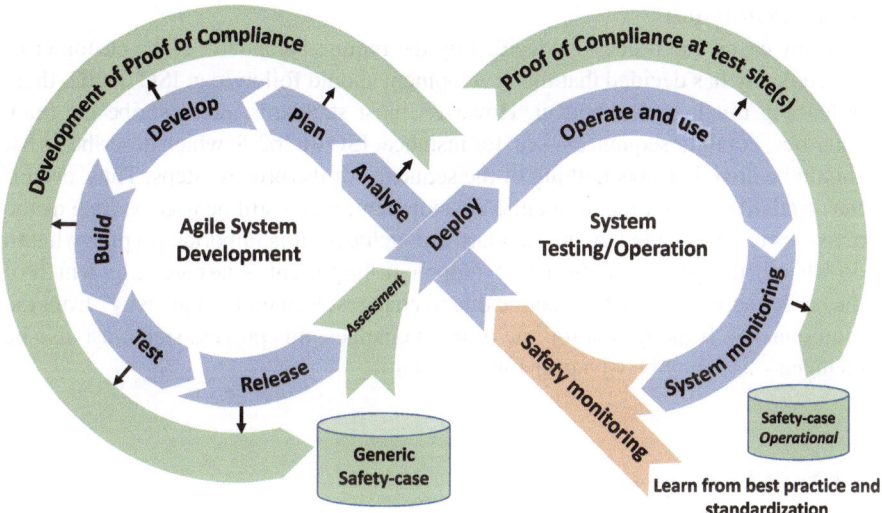

Fig. 10.1 The DevOps process

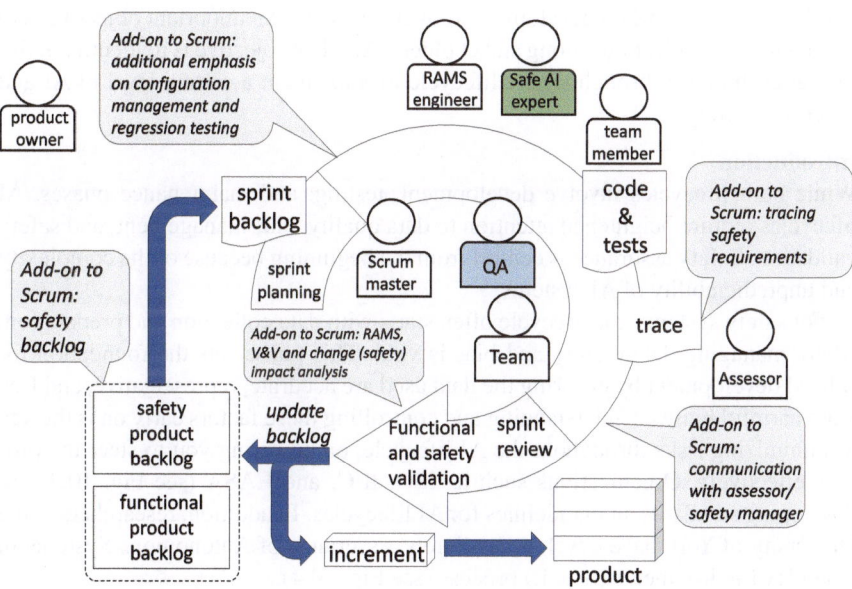

Fig. 10.2 The SafeScrum process

of the waterfall safety lifecycle or V-model that are applied together with the SafeScrum process—see Fig. 10.2. See also Harney et al. (2021). For a complete description of the SafeScum method, see Hanssen et al. (2018).

Safety Plan Issues

In many cases, the process is decided by the required standard. If the customer or the company has decided that the development should follow, e.g. ISO 26262, there is nothing much to do about it. However, most standards just describe the main activities, not their sequence—see, for instance, ISO 26262-8, which describes what should be done but says nothing of the sequence of the process steps. Thus, even if the standard does not mention agile development, it can still be used as long as the activities recommended by the standard are included. It is important to plan what to do when/if things change during development. Important issues are, e.g., which of the earlier activities must be redone due to changes. Remember the "why" from the requirements. If the reason for one of them changes, this process step must also be changed—and may be whatever follows after it.

10.2 AI Lifecycles

Objective

This chapter provides a defined set of safety, software, and AI lifecycle processes that should be used when developing products/systems. An important objective is to facilitate communication among stakeholders. Another objective is to identify activities at each phase throughout the lifecycle to implement a certain level of AI and functional safety.

Introduction

While both lifecycles involve development, testing, and maintenance phases, AI lifecycles require heightened attention to data quality, bias management, and safety validation. Safety assurance is central from the beginning because of the complexity and unpredictability of AI systems.

For safety systems, the lifecycle often starts with data collection and preparation, where managing data quality and bias is vital. This phase sets the foundation for safe AI development by ensuring the data used are accurate, representative, and free from harmful biases. Understanding and controlling these factors early on is the key to minimizing risks throughout the AI lifecycle, empowering you to steer the process effectively. Organizations such as ISO, IEC, and EASA (see Fig. 10.3) are developing standards and guidelines for AI lifecycles. In addition, researchers at the University of York have developed a Safety Assurance of Autonomous Systems in Complex Environments (SACE) process (see Fig. 10.4).

EASA (EASA 34) has developed a W-shaped process model that is an adaptation of the V-shaped development model for machine learning (ML) applications, focusing on development and verification. It starts with managing and verifying requirements, followed by data preparation for training, validation, and evaluation. The process includes managing the learning process, training, and validating the model to ensure it meets performance metrics. The model is then implemented in the target environment, where its accuracy and performance are verified. Finally, independent

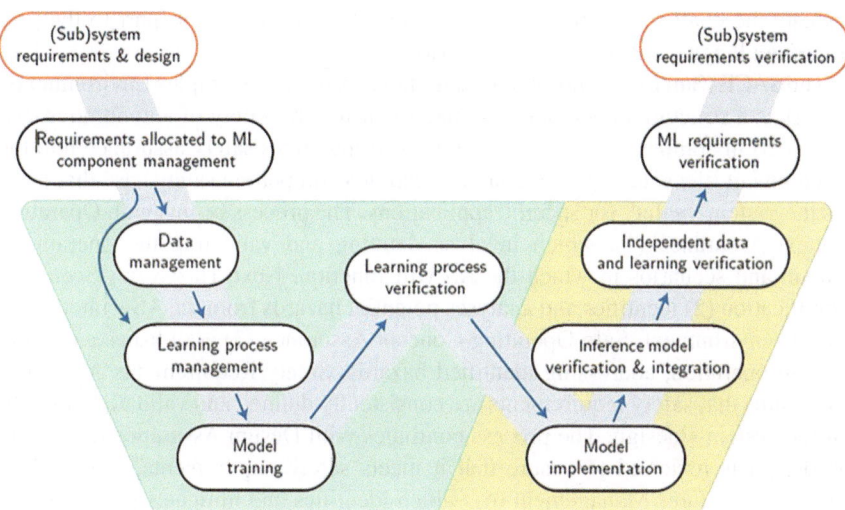

Fig. 10.3 W model by ASA and Daedalean. © (EASA 34)

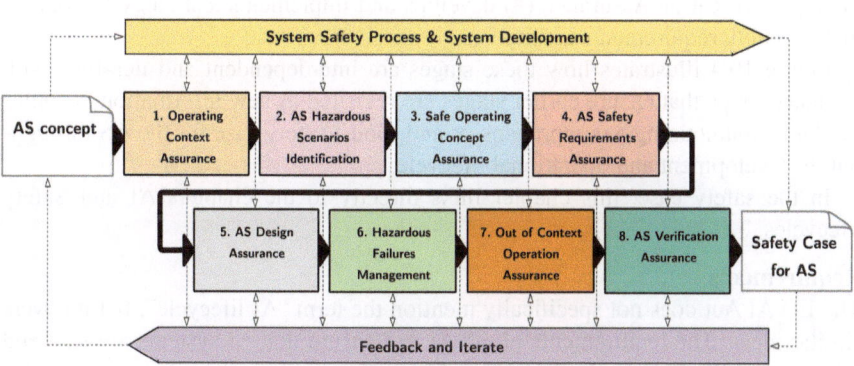

Fig. 10.4 The SACE process developed by © (Hawkins et al. 2022)

data and learning verification ensure adherence to requirements, providing a robust framework for deploying ML models in safety-critical settings.

Carter et al. (2023) describe the role of Python and C++ in the Machine Learning Development Lifecycle (MLDL) and Machine Learning Implementation Lifecycle (MLIL), similar to the W model by EASA. Python is favoured for developing ML models due to its flexibility and extensive libraries, making it a key tool in the MLDL. However, Python's dynamic typing and interpreted nature pose challenges for deployment in safety-critical environments, particularly in the MLIL. For safety-critical applications, one should include, e.g., a transition from Python to a programming language like C++ during the MLIL to ensure reliability and compliance with safety standards. In some of our ongoing projects (Myklebust et al., 2025), we evaluate the challenges when moving from Python in the MLDL part to the programming language Rust in the MLIL part.

The SACE (Safety Assurance of Autonomous Systems in Complex Environments) process is a structured approach designed to ensure the safety of autonomous systems (AS) in complex and dynamic settings. It integrates safety assurance into the development lifecycle, with the goal of creating a compelling safety case that justifies the system's safety for specific applications. The process begins with Operating Context Assurance (1), which involves defining and validating the operational domain and scenarios in which the AS will function. Next, Hazardous Scenarios Identification (2) identifies and analyses potential hazards from the AS's interaction with its environment. Safe Operating Concept Assurance (3) establishes a concept for safe operation, addressing identified hazards. Safety Requirements Assurance (4) ensures that safety requirements are consistently defined and validated throughout the system's design. The process continues with Design Assurance (5), where the design is reviewed to ensure that it meets safety requirements, followed by Hazardous Failures Management (6), which identifies and mitigates potential failures during operation. Out of Context Operation Assurance (7) addresses the AS's behaviour when operating outside its defined context, ensuring safe transitions. Finally, Verification Assurance (8) develops and implements a strategy to confirm that all safety requirements are met.

Figure 10.4 illustrates how these stages are interdependent and iterative, with feedback loops that ensure earlier stages are revisited as new information becomes available, maintaining a comprehensive and robust safety case for the AS throughout its development and operational lifecycle.

In the safety case, this chapter links directly to the chapters AI and Safety lifecycles.

Requirements
The EU AI Act does not specifically mention the term "AI lifecycle", but it covers similar ideas. The requirements in the AI Act ensure that AI systems are safe and reliable throughout their development, deployment, and use. The Act sets rules for managing risks, requires ongoing monitoring after AI systems are put on the market, and holds developers responsible for compliance at every stage. This way, the Act indirectly addresses the entire lifecycle of AI systems.

The Blue Guide (EA, 2022) defines and describes different approaches like "Put on the market", "making available on the market", and "Putting into service".

ISO/IEC 22989:2022 outlines a high-level lifecycle model for AI systems, while ISO/IEC 5338:2023 specifies lifecycle processes for AI systems. The standards ISO/PAS 8800:2024-12 has recently been issued. This PAS defines safety-related properties and risk factors impacting the insufficient performance and malfunctioning behaviour of AI within a road vehicle context. ISO/IEC TR 5469:2024 adds information related to the Relationship between the AI lifecycle and the functional safety lifecycle.

Agile Adaptation
Certain adaptations are necessary to address AI's challenges when developing AI safety systems using agile methodologies. Iterative risk assessment should be integrated into relevant sprints, allowing for continuous evaluation of risks and safety concerns as the AI system evolves. Backlogs, e.g. tagging the safety elements as in SafeScrum, must prioritize safety requirements and risk mitigation alongside functionality, ensuring that safety-related tasks are given sufficient priority. Cross-functional teams should include safety experts who collaborate closely with the developers, ensuring that safety considerations are embedded throughout the development process. Frequent and transparent communication through daily scrum (Myklebust et al., 2018a) about safety concerns is essential, keeping all stakeholders informed and involved in addressing issues.

Safety Plan Issues
Key issues include selecting the appropriate development model and process that aligns with both the project's needs, context, relevant standards, and the product's safety requirements. This involves ensuring that safety considerations are embedded throughout the AI lifecycle, including data collection, model training, verifications, and system validation phases. Continuous risk assessment, iterative evaluation, and adaptation of processes, with a focus on safety, are essential to maintaining compliance with AI and FuSa standards.

Chapter 11
Tools, Programming Languages, and Pre-existing Software

This chapter consists of five sections outlining aspects related to tools, libraries, formats, and programming languages, as well as considerations that need to be made regarding pre-existing software.

11.1   Tools

Objective

The objective of this part of the safety plan is to provide evidence that the use and potential failures of development tools do not adversely affect the output in a safety-related manner that is undetected by technical and/or organizational measures outside the tool.

Information

Tools have become increasingly important when developing safety-critical systems and are of paramount importance when developing high risk AI systems. Evaluating tools has a similar safety case chapter and a safety case reference often named "Software programming languages and SW tools validation".

Requirements

High risk systems must comply with essential requirements, including maintaining a risk management system, ensuring data quality, and providing technical documentation, but the AI Act does not specifically address development tools. See also Chap. 8. The generic standard IEC 61508:2010 includes two types of support tools: offline and online tools. Support tools either support the development of a product or are used to gain confidence in the product. Such tools include product management lifecycle tools, development, requirement, and design tools, language translators, testing, Gen AI and debugging tools, and configuration management tools.

As opposed to EN 50128:2011 and EN 50716:2023, IEC 61508:2010 describes both off-line tools and online tools. Online support tools are software tools that can

© The Author(s) 2025
T. Myklebust et al., *The AI Act and The Agile Safety Plan*, SpringerBriefs in
Computer Science, https://doi.org/10.1007/978-3-031-80504-2_11

directly influence the safety-related system during its run time, e.g. online diagnostic tests. If the online tool can affect the AI system, it should normally only affect the non-safety part of the system. Off-line software tools support one or more AI/safety phases or activities of the software development lifecycle. They cannot directly influence the safety-related system during its run time.

EN 50128:2011 section 3.1.42–3.1.43, EN 50716:2023 section 6.7.4, and IEC 61508-4:2010 section 3.2.11 define three categories for tools used in software development, copy from EN 50128:2011:

- **T1**: *generates no outputs which directly or indirectly can contribute to the executable code (including data) of the safety related system, e.g. text editor or configuration control tool.*
- **T2**: *supports the test or verification of the design or executable code, where errors in the tool can fail to reveal defects but cannot directly create errors in the executable software. E.g. test harness generator or static analysis tool.*
- **T3**: *generates output, which directly or indirectly can contribute to the executable code (including data) of the safety related system. E.g. optimizing compiler where the relationship between the source code program and the generated object code is not obvious or a compiler that incorporates an executable runtime package into the executable code.*

When tools are used to replace manual operations, the same process steps can be used to demonstrate evidence of the integrity of tools' output as if the output was done in manual operation. If we can provide convincing arguments for the integrity of the tool's output and the integrity level of the software, according to relevant AI and safety standards, it is not decreased by the tool replacement, these process steps might be replaced by alternative methods.

Tools of categories T2 and T3 will need some kind of assurance that they will not create safety problems. If we cannot assure the assessors and ourselves that tools of categories T2 and T3 are safe, we might need to reconsider our tool use and thus update the safety plan for the whole project.

Agile Adaptations The Agile Manifesto from 2001 states, "*Individuals and interactions over processes and tools*", clearly indicating an underestimation of the importance of tools. We think that this is probably the least future-oriented statement of the manifesto. Tools are important, especially when taking an agile approach, as more tests have to be performed. And when more frequent deliveries are expected, it is crucial to have tools for most of the processes and tests.

Due to general SW development and AI, we suggest that the agile manifesto should be changed to:

Individuals and interactions, including processes and several tools

Satisfying the safety plan means to satisfy regulators—follow the rules—and the customer—realize the requirements. Two tools are of paramount importance

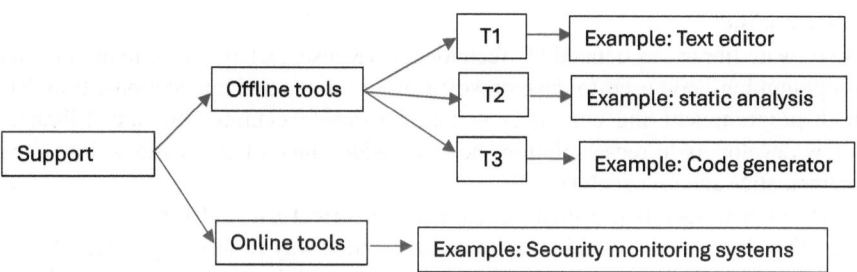

Fig. 11.1 Support tools and classifications

- One needed to satisfy the traceability requirements
- One needed to test the fulfilment of the functional requirements

Neither activity is normally doable without tool support. This is true both for agile projects and for any other development model.

Testing is important in all software development and even more so in agile development, due to the frequent changes in the code. Tests function as a safety net that supports code changes—test, change, and then test again. Without a large set of test cases, the probability of introducing new errors during changes would be too high. However, the test—change—test approach requires the developers to run a large set of tests quite often, which would be next to impossible without a testing tool allowing a large degree of test automation. The tool should allow automated executions and correctness check of the tests.

Safety Plan Issues
It is important to gain an overview of the relevant tools, libraries, and formats early. Hence, the main parts of the "Programming language and tools validation plan" should be developed early, if not already established, as part of an earlier project.

The safety plan needs to contain tool identifications—which tools are we going to use? How are we going to use them? The latter include things such as scripts and templates. In addition, we need to categorize (which class T1, etc.; see Fig. 11.1) and, in some cases, certify the tools we use, depending on what they are used for.

11.2   Libraries

Objectives
This part of the safety plan's objective is to provide evidence that potential software library failures do not adversely affect the output in a safety-related manner, undetected by technical and/or organizational measures outside the library, in compliance with the AI Act's requirements for high risk AI systems regarding safety, robustness, and transparency.

Information

A software library, as defined by Technopedia (Rouse, 2016), is a suite of data and programming code used to develop software programs and applications. It assists both programmers and compilers in building and executing software. Libraries allow developers to reuse solutions across a wide range of applications, including mathematics and text analysis.

Developers face two primary challenges: incorrect use and version discrepancies. Developers may use a library in an unintended way to solve a problem. When the library is updated, these workarounds can fail. Additionally, developers and customers may use different library versions, leading to compatibility issues. Libraries may also vary depending on the operating system and hardware, adding complexity. However, a survey of 13 Norwegian software companies shows that libraries are not a major source of software errors (Stålhane & Johnsen, 2019) (Fig. 11.2).

Some libraries lack maintenance, making it hard to know if they are updated. If trust in a library erodes, switching to a new one can be costly. New libraries may also offer better functionality. Libraries are also used for testing applications, such as PractiTest (2024) and "The Industrial Self-Test Library" for IEC 61508. Even if they are not included in delivery, these libraries need periodic updates.

Release managers notice frequent library changes, often due to new security fixes. Companies must decide if these fixes are necessary, balancing security concerns with marketplace image. Security focus has increased library maintenance costs.

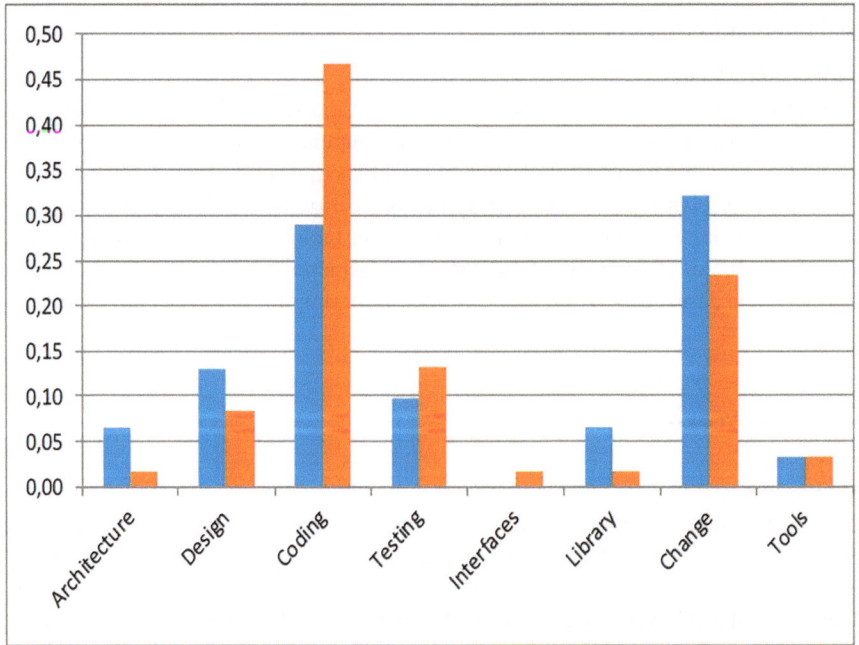

Fig. 11.2 Knowledge-based problem areas identified by software developers (blue: safety and security, orange: other) (Stålhane & Johnsen, 2019)

There are two choices when integrating libraries into a system: include libraries in the delivery or assume that the customer possesses the libraries. Including libraries in the delivery is safer but carries the risk of missing out on newer versions.

When purchasing a software system:

- Verify the libraries used, review the update history, and examine the update details
- Identify all explicitly and indirectly included libraries, determine when and by whom libraries were updated, and understand the source and purpose of updates

For certified systems, all libraries must be part of the certification, which can be challenging if maintained by volunteers.

This topic has a similar safety case chapter, and a safety case reference often named "Software programming languages and SW tools validation".

Requirements
High risk systems must comply with essential requirements, including maintaining a risk management system, ensuring data quality, and providing technical documentation. Still, the AI Act does not specifically address libraries.

IEC 61508:2010 addresses libraries broadly, emphasizing trustable reusable software components. Key criteria include stable specifications, evidence of usage, operating history, and documented procedures for fault management.

ISO 26262:2018 is more practical, focusing on the contract with suppliers and detailed qualification requirements, such as specifications, resource needs, runtime environment requirements, API descriptions, and error handling.

ISO 26262-8:2018 clause 12, "Qualification of software components", mentions libraries in an example: *"software libraries from third-party suppliers commercial off-the-shelf (COTS) software"*.

The more pragmatic ISO/PAS 8926:2024, "Road vehicles Functional safety Use of pre-existing software architectural elements", could also be consulted.

Agile Adaptations The use of libraries should be aligned with the tool adaptations described above.

Safety Plan Issues
It is important to gain an overview of the relevant libraries early. If not already established, the main parts of the "Programming language and tools validation plan" should be developed early as part of an earlier project.

11.3 Formats

Objectives
This part of the safety plan's objective is to provide evidence that potential format failures do not adversely affect the output in a safety-related manner that is undetected by technical and/or organizational measures outside the format.

Information

The IEEE P2851.1 "Standard for the Enablement of Functional Safety Interoperability with Reliability" and IEC 61784-3:2021 "Industrial communication networks—Profiles—Part 3: Functional safety fieldbuses—General rules and profile definitions" are two of the few standards that include relevant information about formats and related topics.

The expansion of automated driving and autonomous mobile robotics drives the rapid growth of formats and annotations as part of safety-critical systems. However, there are currently no standardized methods, languages, or formats for exchanging safety-related data on reliability aspects like Base Failure Rate (BFR), Soft Error Rate (SER), System RAS (Reliability, Availability, and Serviceability), and Prognostics. This lack of standardization forces companies to spend excessive time and effort on reconciling, comparing, integrating, and combining diverse data formats and annotations, leading to inefficiencies and increased risks. Serviceability is the ease with which a system can be maintained and repaired. Effective serviceability ensures quick resolution of issues, minimizing downtime and maintaining system integrity.

The IEEE P2851 committee addresses the need for standardized methods, languages, and formats to facilitate data exchange related to these aspects. They aim to accelerate the safety engineering process, reduce risks and costs, and enable tool interoperability.

One objective of IEEE P2851.1 is to define a format for exchanging and interoperability safety-related analysis and verification activities, promoting consistency in results delivery. IEC 61784-3:2021 provides principles for transmitting safety-relevant messages within distributed networks using fieldbus technology, based on the black channel approach, in line with IEC 61508 for functional safety.

By adopting these standards, we can streamline the development of safety-critical systems, ensuring reliable, available, and serviceable solutions. This topic has a similar safety case chapter, and a safety case reference often named "Software programming languages and SW tools validation".

Requirements

IEC 61508:2010 addresses formats weakly, emphasizing trustable reusable software components. Key criteria include stable specifications, evidence of usage, operating history, and documented procedures for fault management. IEC 61784-3:2021 is referenced by IEC 61508-2:2010. This standard presents, among other things, Protocol Data unit format and Data Link Protocol Data Unit.

ISO 26262-8:2018 clause 12 *"Qualification of software components"* addresses software components.

Preferably, the more pragmatic IEEE P2851™-2023 (STD22) standard could also be consulted. ISO TR 4804 refers to the IEEE P2851.1. ISO TR 4804 will soon be replaced by ISO/CD TS 5083 *"Road vehicles—Safety for automated driving systems—Design, verification and validation"*.

Agile Adaptations

Formats should be aligned with the tool adaptations described above.

Safety Plan Issues

It is important to gain an overview of the relevant formats early. The main parts of the "Programming language and tools validation plan" should be developed early, if not already established, as part of an earlier project.

11.4   Programming Languages

Objective

The objective of this part of the safety plan is to ensure that the programming languages chosen should lead to easily verifiable code with a minimum of effort and facilitate program development, verification, and maintenance. Serviceability, as described in IEEE P2851™-2023 (STD22), could also be evaluated.

Information

Programming language (PL) requirements are part of all functional safety standards, but they have not defined what a programming language is. ISO/IEC/IEEE 24765:2017 has defined programming language as 1: a language used to express computer programs and 2: an artificial language for expressing programs. This topic has a similar safety case chapter, and a safety case reference often named "Software programming languages and SW tools validation".

Requirements

In short, the PL should support defensive programming, strong typing, structured programming, and assertions and enable easy code verification and maintenance. ISO/IEC 5469:2024 does not include much information relating to PLs but includes "Interpretation for AI system technology elements" of Table A.3 "Interpretation of software design and development—support tools and programming language" in IEC 61508-3:2010. IEC 61508:2010 and EN 50128:2011 require PLs, including the presentation of named PLs. "New" safety standards such as ISO 26262:2018 and EN 50716:2023 include requirements without specifying named PLs like C++. We consider this a better approach, as many companies have started using RUST, which is not mentioned in the safety standards. IEC 61508-3 draft 2024 refers to ISO/IEC TR 24772, which provides an example of documenting language vulnerabilities as expected in a safety manual. It is also important to be aware of the reduced number of requirements when using limited variable language/programs (LVL), e.g. IEC 61508:2010-3, chapter G.4, and IEC 61511-1:2016. LVL can be used as part of the SafeScrum process (Myklebust et al., 2016b).

Agile Adaptation

When applying an agile approach, normally more tools are used by the manufacturers. Therefore, choosing programming languages that support AI and safety requirements is crucial. Additionally, integrating robust static analysis tools, formal methods, and automated testing within iterative agile processes ensures ongoing verification and compliance with safety standards while maintaining thorough documentation and traceability.

Safety Plan Issues

Early tool evaluations are important to ensure that the best programming languages are used.

In our experience, too many manufacturers start too late to develop the "Software programming languages and SW tools validation" document.

11.5   Pre-existing Software

Objective

The objective of this part of the safety plan for pre-existing software is to ensure that it fulfils the allocated requirements, detects any potential failures, and integrates seamlessly into the system without compromising safety. This includes a thorough validation process, precise documentation of functions and constraints, and an emphasis on using verified software components wherever possible.

Information

Several factors affect the usefulness, value, and quality of pre-existing products. Pre-existing products can also be presented as COTS products and several other acronyms and names. While useful in many instances, there are several factors that need to be considered when applying pre-existing products.

The products should preferably be SILx capable and have a safety case. If they do not have a safety case, they should include a certificate and a corresponding certificate report. In addition, the safety case or the certificate should state which relevant AI and safety standards the product complies with. In the EU/EEA, a product that is CE Marked has to comply with several regulations and directives, e.g. the AI Act (Regulation 2024/1689), ElectroMagnetic Compatibility (EMC) directive, Cyber Resilience Act (CRA), and Radio Equipment Directive (RED). Maritime products could preferably have a wheel mark. Safety products, e.g. SEooC, should include a safety manual according to IEC 61508.

This topic has a similar safety case chapter. Relevant safety case references are the work products listed in ISO/PAS 8926:2024 "Road vehicles functional safety use of pre-existing software architectural elements":

- Impact analysis
- Safety plan
- SW safety requirements (refined)
- Hardware–software interface (HSI) specification (refined)
- SW architectural design specification (refined)
- Safety-oriented analysis report
- SW verification specification (refined)
- SW verification report (refined)
- Change report

Requirements

The EU AI Act addresses the integration and compliance of pre-existing software by requiring detailed technical documentation that includes information on software interactions and version updates. High risk AI systems must undergo conformity assessments to ensure they meet regulatory requirements, and any significant modifications to pre-existing software necessitate a new assessment. This ensures that AI systems remain compliant with safety and performance standards even after software updates. Preferably, the more pragmatic ISO/PAS 8926:2024 could also be consulted.

Agile Adaptation

When integrating pre-existing software into safety-critical systems using agile methodologies, it is crucial to ensure incremental validation and integration, maintaining precise documentation of functions, constraints, safety cases, and compliance with AI and safety standards and the EU AI Act. Continuous impact analysis during relevant sprint by the "alongside engineering"/RAMS team should assess the effects of integrating pre-existing software on overall system safety and functionality. Automated testing and verification, including static and dynamic analysis, are essential to meet safety-critical requirements.

Safety Plan Issues

Early evaluations of pre-existing software are important to ensure that the best software is used.

Validation is important to meet all requirements and integrate seamlessly without compromising safety. It should include precise documentation of functions, constraints, safety cases, and compliance with standards. Regular impact analysis during dedicated sprints should assess the integration effects on system safety and functionality. Automated testing and verification, including static and dynamic analysis, are crucial to detect potential failures and ensure reliability. The plan should also ensure that all pre-existing software components have the necessary safety information to demonstrate compliance.

Chapter 12
Hazards and Risks

This chapter consists of four sections outlining how to deal with hazards and ongoing risk management. First, we elaborate on how to approach an analysis of a system's hazards and implement and maintain a hazard log. Next, we elaborate on how ongoing risk management and dynamic risk analysis should ensure that high risk systems are under continuous monitoring and regular review. In the process of hazard identification and risk management, having clearly formulated risk tolerability criteria is paramount. Therefore, Sect. 12.3 outlines several approaches one could use for this purpose. When addressing a high risk system's possible hazards and risk management strategies, it is important to also ensure the effective management and integration of the specific rules, limitations, and constraints that must be followed and monitored when using the system. The last section therefore outlines on safety-related application conditions (SRAC).

12.1 Hazard Identification and Analysis

Objective
The purpose of hazard identification and analysis is to understand and identify how the proposed system may cause harm to persons, the equipment, the operation, or the environment.

Introduction
There are several ways to analyse a system's hazards, depending on the state of the development or maintenance process—i.e. what information is available (Myklebust & Stålhane, 2018)

- Early in the development process we recommend the two methods PHA (Preliminary Hazard Analysis) and HazID (Hazard Identification). They are simple to use, which allows us to include customers and developers in the process.

© The Author(s) 2025
T. Myklebust et al., *The AI Act and The Agile Safety Plan*, SpringerBriefs in
Computer Science, https://doi.org/10.1007/978-3-031-80504-2_12

- The HazOp method is more complex but can be used in all phases of system development. The method is heavy on ceremony and requires an experienced process leader. The method applies a set of guide words, also called deviations, to cue in the process participants on possible hazards for each system element.

The hazard analysis process serves as the basis for establishing a hazard log; in those cases, a hazard log is not already established as part of previous project. Throughout the hazard analysis process, it is important to use the information found in the hazard log (Hanssen et al., 2018). The hazard log is constructed based on earlier experiences plus the initial hazard identification and safety analysis. New hazards will be added to the log as they appear, due to, e.g., new or changed requirements, changes to the system's planned operating environment, or the discovery of a new hazard, for instance during a daily stand-up or during a sprint review.

Requirements
The Articles 6 "Classification rules for high risk AI systems", 9 "Risk management system", 10 "Data and data governance" and 15 "Accuracy, robustness and cybersecurity" together with Annex III "High risk AI systems referred to in Article 6(2)" should be consulted. See also Chap. 8.

All safety standards require hazard and safety analysis. In order to perform a hazard analysis, there are four sine qua non: a deep understanding of

- The system's role in operation
- The system's behaviour for every input—I know that is a tall order
- The system's operating environment—the ODD
- How the system and its ODD interact

It is important to use methods that allow the involvement of developers, users, and other stakeholders since these groups have important knowledge related to possible hazards—either their cause or their consequences. Once the hazards and their causes have been identified, it is important to agree on what to do to prevent their occurrence. This may be related to the system—e.g. data output control—or to the environments—e.g. physical barriers.

Identifying hazards and deciding how to prevent them from happening are the most important inputs to the system's safety case. The following two claims are important parts of the safety case:

- We have identified all relevant hazards because…
- All identified hazards are handled in a safe and reliable way—see …

Agile Adaptation
As always, agile adaptations relate to handling changes to requirements, ODD, ConOps, or system implementation. However, remember that changes will occur—agility or not. What separates agile development from the rest is that we are planning for change and will handle it in a controlled manner (Hanssen et al., 2018). For an AI system, it is also important to consider changes to the training dataset. Any change in hazard analysis should initiate a CIA—Change Impact Analysis (Hanssen et al., 2018). The purpose of this analysis is to identify the influence the changes have on the hazard analysis—i.e. has it introduced new hazards, do we have to

change the way we defend against one or more hazards, and so on. During the change impact analysis, it is also important to update the hazard log if new hazard possibilities are found. See also Department of Defence (DoD) hazard tracking process (Myklebust et al., 2020).

Safety Plan Issues

Hazard identification and how we handle it are important inputs to the safety case. Thus, there might be documents that are not part of the system delivery but are still important to the safety case arguments. If we have an AI system, one important document is the documentation of the training dataset.

12.2 Ongoing Risk Management, Dynamic Risks, and Emergencies

Objective

The purpose of the ongoing risk management, dynamic risk analysis, and emergencies chapter is to understand and identify changing risk situations and their possible causes.

Introduction

First and foremost, we need to define three terms

- Ongoing risk management: Continuous monitoring and regular review of risks are crucial for adapting to new challenges and changes in project scope, environment, or objectives.
- A dynamic risk is a risk brought on by sudden and unpredictable changes in the economy or, e.g., sudden changes in the environment.
- An emergency is an urgent, unexpected, and usually dangerous situation that poses an immediate risk to health, life, property, or the environment, requiring immediate action.

Before we go any further, it is important to reiterate on five important points from The Food and Drug Administration's guide (FDA, 2002):

- Software does not wear out. The defect was designed in.
- Software fails without warning. There are no such things as intermittent failures.
- Software can be more complex than hardware.
- Software is changed too easily.
- Seemingly insignificant changes in one area of software functionality can lead to disastrous defects in unrelated areas of functionality.

It is important to be aware that the occurrence of some of the hazards will not depend on the state of the software alone but also on

- Events or states of the software's operating environment—the ODD.

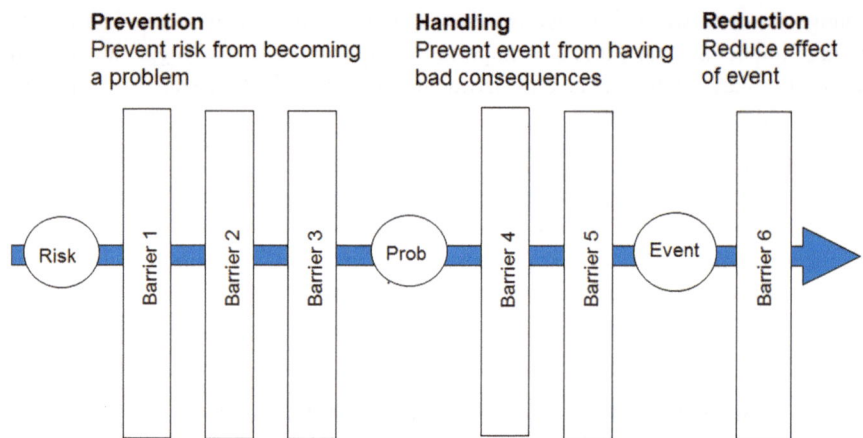

Fig. 12.1 From risk to accident—the barrier model

- The efficiency of the barriers used to prevent a risk from becoming an accident. Note that barriers may be placed in the software, in the operating instructions, in the system under control, or in a remote operations centre.

Such connections need to be identified and followed up in the ongoing risk management (Fig. 12.1).

Bear in mind not all of these barriers need to be inside the software. This holds for the handling barriers and especially for the "Reduction" barrier(s) which almost always are physical.

Requirements

Regarding AI Act requirements, see Sect. 12.1 above.

The issues raised by the FDA guide may be turned into the following three requirements:

- When a hazard is identified and we have decided how to avoid or control it, then for each ODD or SW change, we need to check that the hazard is still under control.
- A hazard analysis will run into a situation where we see that event X is not hazardous now but if it changes to event Y it might be dangerous. If this is the case, we need to keep a watch on event X. The safety case defeating arguments will also fit in here.
- We need to keep track of the connection between hazard events and the ODD. Any change in the ODD may lead to the need to check on the hazard analysis.

As stated in the introduction, "Dynamic risk" is an economic term and is used in managing a company's economy. However, "sudden and unpredictable changes" can happen anywhere, also in an ODD. Thus, it is important to be able to observe sudden changes in the ODD, analyse the effect to see if any new hazards are introduced, and identify how the system shall cope with them.

When it comes to emergencies, the handling will depend on the situation and environment. UL 4600:2023 (STD50) requires some unconventional (not typically found on a conventional vehicle) devices such as autonomous mode indicator, vehicle-disabled indicator, and microphone for picking up emergency vehicle sirens. IMO requirements covering, e.g., machinery and electrical installations are designed to ensure that services that are essential for the safety of the ship, passengers, and crew are maintained under various emergency conditions.

Agile Adaptation
SafeScrum has already introduced an extra activity for the stand-ups—always ask "Have you done anything that might influence the system's safety?" However, the concept of "ongoing risk management" requires that the safety question now needs a much wider interpretation of the system's safety. It will include operators, the physical system under control of the software, and its physical environment.

As a consequence of this, the stand-up meetings—or at least some of them— must include a much wider group of participants. We are aware that this might be impractical, but it is still necessary if you want to adapt the principle of ongoing risk management. It is also important when you want to handle dynamic risks. An alternative could be to include the wider group of participants and the "ongoing risk management" only to the sprint reviews, where the customer, at least in theory, shall participate.

Safety Plan Issues
In order to be able to handle emergencies related to the system and its ODD, we first need to define system safe states—if any—and emergency indicators. If a possible emergency is indicated, the system should be programmed to do three things:

- Move the system to a safe state
- Activate possible alarms
- Contact personnel that can handle the relevant emergencies—e.g. medics, firefighters, or rescue personnel. It is important that the persons contacted receive as much relevant information as possible.

The issues discussed under "Requirements" require documenting relationships between hazard analysis, Con-Ops, ODD, and software and keeping these documents up-to-date. It is also important to decide when to include the customer and domain experts and make plans and agreements for their process inclusion.

12.3   Risk Tolerability Criteria

Objective
The purpose of the risk tolerability criteria chapter is to understand and identify how to balance risks and benefits. Risk tolerability criteria are crucial in maintaining acceptable levels of risk throughout the lifecycle of these systems, with continuous

monitoring and human oversight playing significant roles in their implementation and enforcement.

Introduction

It is important to keep the two concepts "risk acceptance criteria" and "system acceptance criteria" separated. The system acceptance criteria are a set of concrete events which, when they occur, will lead the stakeholders to accept the system. The risk acceptance criteria say something about the risk level that we are willing to accept and are a question of cost vs. benefits.

In order to discuss risk tolerability, we need to identify what the risks are, introduce risk reducing measures, and thereby improve the situation (Haugen & Rausand, 2011). In the end, two conflicting objectives need to be balanced:

- We want to do everything possible to remove all risks.
- Often it is not practical to remove all risk.

    The question is then:

- How much risk should we remove before we stop?
- How do we balance risk and benefits?

The level where we stop is defined by an acceptance criterion. The remaining risk or residual risk is the risk that remains after we have introduced relevant measures. Although there are several methods available to deal with this issue, we will use the As Low As Reasonably Practicable (ALARP) concept, mainly because it is simple to understand and simple to use. Those who want to look at a heavier method should consult MEM—Minimal Endogenous Mortality or GALE—Globally At Least Equivalent (Risk Engineering, 2024). Note that in order to use the GALE method, you will need something to compare your system to—e.g. the system that you plan to replace. See also EU (2024f)—Common Safety Methods.

Requirements

Article 9 of the AI Act addresses the need for a comprehensive risk management system for high risk AI systems. This includes identifying, estimating, evaluating, and managing known and reasonably foreseeable risks to health, safety, and fundamental rights, including those from foreseeable misuse. The article also states that residual risk must be evaluated and judged as "acceptable", echoing principles like As Low As Reasonable Practicable (ALARP), where risks must be reduced as far as reasonably practicable. See also Sect. 12.1 above. To use the ALARP model, we normally need to define the three regions, "broadly acceptable", "tolerable", and "unacceptable". The HSE's recommendation to the nuclear industry was (HMSO, 1992):

- "Broadly acceptable" threshold to be one in a million (10-6) per year
- "Limit of tolerability" threshold to be

    - One in a thousand (10-3) per year for voluntary employees.
    - One in ten thousand (10-4) per year for the public who have the risk imposed on them "in the wider interest of society".

		Hazard probability				
		Frequent	**Probable**	**Occasional**	**Remote**	**Improbable**
Severity	Catastrophic	High	High	High	High	Medium
	Critical	High	High	High	Medium	Low
	Marginal	High	Medium	Medium	Low	Low
	Negligible	Medium	Low	Low	Low	Low

Fig. 12.2 Risk acceptance categories

An alternative is using a probability–consequence/severity table like the one shown below. The MIL-STD-882E:2012 standard also contains definitions of the terms used, e.g. "frequent" and "intolerable" (Fig. 12.2).

In any case, calibration needs to be in terms of the particular risks. For factory workers whose equipment risks may be of damage to a hand, or of impairment to hearing, it may be in terms of the acceptable and intolerable numbers of accidents per worker per year. In the case of risks to the environment, losses are, typically, expressed in financial terms—though there are difficulties in credibly determining these because, in many cases, market values do not apply (Redmill, 2010).

The system often will undergo change—agility or not. Thus, it is important to document the relationship between code behaviour and its effect on the ODD. A simple FMEA, updated for each system change, combined with good ODD-knowledge will be a good start. An FMEA with the two failure modes "wrong output" and "no output" will cover most situations.

Agile Adaptation

For any development process the risk tolerability criteria is decided by considering the system, the stakeholders, and the ODD. The agile development process with its frequent communication opportunities—daily stand-ups—will make it possible to discuss the consequences for system risks. The hazard log and other experience reports will be an important input here.

In order to better understand the consequences of a change or adding a new piece of code, it is important to understand the ODD and which unintended system behaviour will cause which type of accident.

Safety Plan Issues

Our understanding of the system's environment will increase over time. Thus, plan to update the ODD description and the FMEA regularly; otherwise it will soon be outdated. If the updating is not in the plan it will not happen.

The whole process, both in "Requirements" and in" Plan issues and topics", will run counter to the credo of agile development where we claim "Code, not documents". However, the requirements to risk tolerability make the extra process steps and documentation necessary.

12.4   Safety-Related Application Conditions, SRAC, and Similar Information

Objective

The objective of this safety plan is to ensure the effective management and integration of SRAC in the development, deployment, and operation of high risk systems. This plan aims to mitigate risks by defining and implementing necessary rules, conditions, and constraints to maintain functional safety across various applications. Additionally, it includes requirements for continuous safety monitoring, maintenance, and decommissioning to ensure ongoing compliance and safety integrity.

Introduction

SRAC is explained in EN 50129 (railway std), but due to AI we had to develop a new explanation: Safety-related application conditions are the specific rules, limitations, and constraints that must be followed and observed when using the system. During development, they can be transferred between the safety and AI phases. They are implemented to minimize the risk of harm or injury to stakeholders and the environment when using the system.

SRAC is also known as "exported risk", "transferred risk", and "passed on risk". Similar requirements are also known as "Instruction of use" [AI Act], Safety note [IEC/IEEE 82079-1], and "information for use". SRACS are an important part of safety management as they can also be used to limit a system to ensure that it is first an assistant system. As a result, it can be classified as a limited system according to the AI Act (regulation 2024/1689). Later, the system can be improved, become a decision system, and then be classified as high risk. In addition, one normally limits the use, site-specific conditions, operational parts, and the ODD.

The stakeholders (installer, maintainer, operator, user) must fully understand each of the SRACS (risk) being exported. It is mandatory to invest time in ensuring that all stakeholders fully understand each of the **SRACs** that should be taken care of.

SRAC is often a separate document and a section in the safety case.

Requirements

The AI Act defines "Instructions for use" as the information provided by the provider to inform the deployer of, in particular, an AI system's intended purpose and proper use. See also Chap. 15.

It is only EN 50129 that explicitly requires an SRAC approach. Since EN 50129 does not include AI, we have improved the SRAC approach:

When developing a safety plan, one should consider including the following sections to ensure adequate SRAC coverage of

- Development. When moving to new AI and safety phases, it is also important to include this as part of, e.g., the DIA or other similar contracts with suppliers and subcontractors.
- Operational. Operational and maintenance safety aspects. And also, e.g., shutdowns or other special causes.

- Maintenance. Relevant safety information related to first-line and second-line maintenance. Modularity and interchangeability.
- Decommissioning. Appropriate safety information related to, e.g., the final disposal or for reuse.

The AI Act (Regulation 2024/1689) includes Annex IV "Technical documentation", which refers to Article 11 "Technical documentation". This Annex includes several requirements including

- 1 (h) instructions for use for the deployer, and a basic description of the user interface provided to the deployer, where applicable;

Other articles that include similar requirements are:

- Article 13: Transparency and provision of information to deployers
- Article 23: Obligations of importers
- Article 24: Obligations of distributors
- Article 26: Obligations of deployers of high risk AI systems
- Article 27: Fundamental rights impact assessment for high risk AI systems

IEC/IEEE 82079-1:2019 "Preparation of information for use (instructions for use) of products Part 1: Principles and general requirements" includes relevant information regarding "safety notes" and "instructions for use" for products.

Each SRAC shall be linked to at least one hazard. As mentioned earlier, there should be a link between the SRS and the HL; this could be e.g. found as part of Requirement Hazard Analysis (RHA) (Myklebust & Stålhane, 2021).

Agile Adaptation

There are several reasons to include an agile approach when including an SRAC or similar approach. One of the main reasons for start-ups and SMEs (small and medium-sized enterprises) is Time To Market (TTM). The SRAC approach can then be combined with incremental development by including SRACs to limit the use and clearly inform the stakeholders.

In addition, this can be part of the strategy. Manufacturers can combine the SRAC approach with the functioning of the system to be developed, starting, e.g., with developing an assistant system that can be classified as a limited risk according to the AI act (regulation 2024/1689) and, e.g., an SAE level 1 or 2 (J3016). Later, they can develop high risk systems, e.g. systems having SAE levels 3–5. SRACs may also be instrumental for manufacturers to ensure that stakeholders really understand the relevant safety aspects of the system.

Safety Plan Issues

This depends on the domain, as the Railway domain mainly uses SRAC. Other domains do not include an approach that is equally clear and explicit. In other domains, IEC/IEEE 82079-1:2022 could be used if not including the SRAC approach.

Early awareness and creation of SRACS to ensure that the SRAC can be handled appropriately and be transferred to the relevant phase and/or stakeholder.

SRACS could also be part of the DIA (ISO 26262-8:2018). The "acceptance of conditions" part of the DIA could preferably be specifically related to SRACs.

Liability issues can be challenging (Widen & Koopman, 2023). An SRAC approach could both help the manufacturer and clarify requirements for relevant stakeholders like drivers of cars and operators.

Chapter 13
Requirements

This chapter first provides insight into safety requirements and how they originate from the hazard analysis or relevant standards. Next, it outlines how to ensure that a system or product's safety is compliant with its functional requirements.

13.1 Adequacy of the Safety Requirements

Objective
The objective is to understand the meaning of adequacy for safety requirements, how to obtain them, and how to keep them adequate throughout the product's lifetime.

Information
There are several interpretations of the term "adequate". That something is *adequate* means that it is

1. Sufficient for a specific need or requirement
2. Good enough
3. Of a quality that is good or acceptable

Lawyers and certification bodies may evaluate "adequate" differently. This is one reason that developing harmonized standards is important.

Requirements
The AI Act, IEC 61508:2010 series, EN 5012X series, and ISO 26262:2018 series use the term "adequate" quite a lot but never bother to define what they mean by it. In this chapter, we will use the first interpretation, meaning that we state that adequate means "sufficient for a specific need or requirement". However, we will not equate need with requirement. Often, the requirements mirror the customers' current needs, while issues such as future needs and adherence to necessary standards and regulations are not included. See also Chap. 8.

© The Author(s) 2025
T. Myklebust et al., *The AI Act and The Agile Safety Plan*, SpringerBriefs in
Computer Science, https://doi.org/10.1007/978-3-031-80504-2_13

For most software systems, there are two sets of safety requirements—the ones resulting from the *hazard analysis* and the ones stated in the *relevant standards*. The first set decides what functionality you should implement in order to be safe. The other set puts requirements on the development process—how to do it and when to do what. The two sets are both necessary in order to make up an adequate set of safety requirements. For both sets of requirements, the ODD is important. Thus, it is important that both are maintained to keep up with changes.

In this context, it is important to note the difference between validation and verification. Validation is the process of checking whether the specification captures the customer's requirements, while verification is the process of checking that the software meets its specifications.

If AI is involved, the ODD definition (see Sect. 3.2) becomes more important, as stated by Cummings et al. (2024): *"The inability of AI to consider unfamiliar variables and relationships not explicitly seen in training is a major barrier to applications on AI in safety-critical settings"*. As a result, improved safety analysis and simulations of, e.g., edge cases are important approaches to ensure a complete requirement specification is achieved.

Agile Adaptation

Using agile development, you will have to deal with three sources of changes to the system:

- Changes to the requirements because the environment has changed or because the customers have gotten a better understanding of the intended functionality or the system's environment
- Changes to the code or its structure—e.g. a new and better algorithm or—Heaven forbid—a new architecture
- Changes in the understanding and interpretation of the requirements

If the requirements or the ODD change, the safety arguments may not be adequate anymore. As also mentioned elsewhere, you will need to keep documentation of relationships between hazard and safety analysis and the ODD. This will be necessary when performing an efficient change impact analysis.

Safety Plan Issues

The plans related to this topic are the plans needed to keep the safety requirements adequate. The information needed to do so will depend on the level of detail—both for the requirements, the ODD, and the test plan. The level of detail in all of these documents will increase over time and this will influence their need to be updated. It is also important to plan for ISO 26262-4:2018 that requires that the architectural design should have an adequate level of granularity.

In an agile development environment, the safety requirements, ODD, and test plan should have an adequate and increasing level of detail over time. This could be done as part of project review or—preferably—as part of the daily stand-up. On the other hand, the daily stand-up can easily turn into a large and boring status meeting, which will destroy the agile development process. We have already suggested including a question related to safety changes during the daily stand-ups. The question related to the adequacy of the safety requirements can easily be included here.

Last but not least—it is important to keep up-to-date on the development of the standards being used and on the interpretations of the EU AI Act.

13.2 Ensuring Compliance with Functional Safety Requirements

Objective

The heading implies that we need to analyse the relationships between:

- The system and the ODD
- The requirements and the intended functionality of the system—do they match?
- The requirements of the system and the safety of persons and environment of the ODD—do the requirements keep people and environment of the ODD out of harm's way?

Information

Safety is always a relationship between what the system does and the system's operating environment—the ODD. Thus, judging whether the system is safe or not involves a thorough understanding of the system, its development process, and its operation within the ODD. For instance, ConOps helps define the intended functions and scenarios under which the system will operate. This includes considerations such as environmental conditions, user interactions, and system limitations. Ensuring safety requires identifying all potential hazards within the ODD and designing mitigation strategies that align with the system's capabilities and constraints.

Compliant means "meeting or in accordance with rules, regulations, or standards". In our case, the rule to be compliant with is that the system shall be safe within the defined ODD. This includes both the development process and the system itself. See also Chap. 8.

Requirements

In Chap. 8, we have listed the articles that ensure the system complies with its functional safety requirements, including continuous risk management, accuracy, and technical robustness.

Several standards—e.g. IEC 61508, EN 50126, and ISO 26262—define a set of needed activities during development depending on the criticality of possible hazards. The three standards mentioned use consequence of malfunction to define (A) SIL (Automotive) Safety Integrity Level. This again gives us a set of activities that should be performed in order to conform to the required level of hazard avoidance— i.e. safety. These standards require that the operational environment (ODD) is considered in the analysis and assignment of the necessary (A)SIL. Consequently, changes to the ODD might lead to a new (A)SIL and thus to a changed set of process requirements. The diagram in Table 13.2.1 shows how the SIL is defined in IEC 61508.

In order to ensure, e.g., the safety of Advanced Driver Assistance Systems (ADAS) and Autonomous Driving (AD) systems, it is important to incorporate the changing nature of interactions between the system and the environment, in the safety analysis process for ADAS and AD systems (Khastgir et al., 2017). When the ODD changes we may need to reassess the risk. An increased risk may lead to more or different sensors and thus to the need to change the sensor system to a higher SIL.

Software developed according to IEC 61508 should be able to be used in an automotive setting (ISO 26262) or vice versa. The problems related to this are discussed by Okoh and Myklebust (2024a, 2024b).

There exist several methods and approaches for determining SILx. Below we have listed methods and approaches used and observed as part of our projects:

1. LOPA (Layers of Protection Analysis). LOPA is a widely used method for determining the appropriate SIL for a Safety Instrumented System (SIS). It involves assessing multiple layers of protection, such as alarms, operator actions, and mechanical safeguards. IEC 61511-2:2016, IEC 61511-3:2016, and NOROG 070:2022.
2. Risk graph. A risk graph evaluates factors such as failure likelihood and incident severity to determine SIL. This method is covered in IEC 61508-6:2010.
3. Derogation of responsibility. Some authorities adopt the strictest approach to SIL selection, ensuring compliance with conservative safety standards.
4. Manufacturers' pragmatic approach. Manufacturers may focus on producing SIL3 systems rather than SIL4 when there is limited market demand, balancing safety needs with business considerations.

The railway standard EN 50129 uses a different approach, as shown in the Table 13.2.1. The SIL is defined by the required TFFR—total functional failure rate. The average frequency of Dangerous Failure per Hour (PFH) is based on IEC 61508. The table is an adaptation of Okoh and Myklebust (2024a). Sector-specific standards define the qualitative measures. They are normally listed in the Annexes of the standards.

Earlier versions of the EN 50129 standard also had a SIL 0 entry. SIL 0 was replaced by the term "basic integrity". See Clause 10.2.11 of EN 50126-2:2017 (STD9), titled 'Requirements for Basic Integrity in the Specification and

Table 13.2.1 TFFR, PFH, and SIL, including basic integrity

TFFR	SIL	PFH	SIL qualitative measures
$10^{-9} \leq$ TFFR $\leq 10^{-8}$	4	$10^{-9} \leq$ PFH $\leq 10^{-8}$	These are described in IEC 61508 and sector-specific standards
$10^{-8} \leq$ TFFR $\leq 10^{-7}$	3	$10^{-9} \leq$ PFH $\leq 10^{-8}$	
$10^{-7} \leq$ TFFR $\leq 10^{-6}$	2	$10^{-9} \leq$ PFH $\leq 10^{-8}$	
$10^{-6} \leq$ TFFR $\leq 10^{-5}$	1	$10^{-9} \leq$ PFH $\leq 10^{-8}$	
TFFR $\geq 10^{-5}$	0/basic integrity	NA	

Demonstration of Reliability, Availability, Maintainability, and Safety (RAMS), Part 2: Systems Approach to Safety.

First and foremost, you need to understand the ODD. This implies that you need to

- Communicate with the users' organization to understand and document the current operating environment and any plans to change it in the near future
- Document the relationship between the ODD, the safety requirements, and the (A)SIL induced process requirements.
- Keep track of any changes that will influence the (A)SIL since they may influence the development process.

According to the APOS Guideline for Follow-up of Safety Instrumented Systems (Håbrekke et al., 2023), it is crucial to regularly update failure rates and optimize proof test intervals. A copy of the summary of this report: *"This guideline describes best practice for follow-up of safety instrumented systems (SIS) during operation of a process facility. It covers management of functional safety, operation, maintenance, monitoring, and management of change. Methods for updating failure rates and optimising test intervals are presented."*

Agile Adaptation

The requirements related to (A)SIL defined by the relevant standards will also apply if we use an agile development process. At least Scrum and SafeScrum require interactions with the stakeholders after each sprint. This is an opportunity to discuss and document changes to the ODD and the customer's requirements and then update any plans that are out of step with the current realities.

Safety Plan Issues

The most important issue here is to keep track of all conditions that help us to define the safety requirements, including the (A)SIL level. Any change will require a change impact analysis to see if the change will influence the (A)SIL or the functional safety requirements—including the process requirements.

Finally—be aware of the law of unintended consequences—the idea that actions or decisions can have unforeseen and unintended consequences, often in ways that are not immediately apparent. This can occur because complex systems often have multiple interconnected parts and emerging properties, and a change in one part of the system can have ripple effects that are difficult to predict.

Chapter 14
System Design Plan

This chapter outlines the System Design Plan, which aims to develop a system that meets functional safety and regulatory requirements while ensuring reliability, transparency, and stakeholder satisfaction. It emphasizes the importance of risk management, effective integration of subsystems, and continuous stakeholder engagement to deliver a compliant and trustworthy system design. The chapter also explores agile adaptations and the role of stakeholder feedback in refining the system throughout its development.

Objective

The System Design Plan is used to develop a system that meets all relevant functional safety and regulatory requirements while ensuring high levels of trust, transparency, and stakeholder satisfaction. This will be achieved through rigorous risk management practices and continuous stakeholder engagement. The plan is used to deliver a reliable, safe, and compliant system design that supports the operational needs and regulatory obligations of the organization, fostering trust and ensuring the protection of users and the environment.

Information

The EU AI Act defines "AI System" as *a machine-based system that is designed to operate with varying levels of autonomy and that may exhibit adaptiveness after deployment, and that, for explicit or implicit objectives, infers, from the input it receives, how to generate outputs such as predictions, content, recommendations, or decisions that can influence physical or virtual environments.*

This part of the plan is closely linked to Sect. 18.2 and Chap. 19.

Four terms in this definition are of special importance as part of the topics of this book. "Machine" is only used in functional safety standards directly linked to machine safety, like ISO 13849-1 and IEC 62061. Other standards, such as ISO 26262 and IEC 61508, do not use the term machine.

A "system" as covered by IEC 61508 includes input interface converters, sensors, communication devices, output converters, actuators, and the E/E/PE

© The Author(s) 2025
T. Myklebust et al., *The AI Act and The Agile Safety Plan*, SpringerBriefs in Computer Science, https://doi.org/10.1007/978-3-031-80504-2_14

(electrical/electronic/programmable) device. Chapter 17 describes autonomy, and Sect. 6.1 describes "adaptiveness".

Often, problems occur at the interfaces between subsystems, products, and components, or as a result of integration with adjacent systems. Understanding and addressing interfaces and integration is essential to achieve safe and reliable systems.

Requirements

Several requirements in the AI Act are related to "System design". See Chap. 8 for more information.

The IEC 61508 series includes requirements for system design in all three requirement parts. When integrating subsystems or products, the safety manual should also be a basis for integrating them into a system. A safety manual is required both in part 2 and part 3 of IEC 61508.

The automotive system requirements are presented in ISO 26262-4:2018. This standard lists 11 relevant work products (including the relevant chapter in parenthesis):

1. 6.5.1 Technical safety requirements specification
2. 6.5.2 Technical safety concept
3. 6.5.3 System Architectural Design Specification
4. 6.5.4 Hardware–software interface (HIS) specification
5. 6.5.5 Specification of requirements for production, operation, service, and decommissioning
6. 6.5.6 Verification report for system architectural design, the hardware–software interface (HIS) specification, the specification of requirements for production, operation, service and decommissioning, and the technical safety
7. 6.5.7 Safety analysis report
8. 7.5.1 Integration and test strategy
9. 7.5.2 Integration and Test Report
10. 8.5.1 Safety validation specification, including safety validation environment description
11. 8.5.2 Safety validation report

When subcontractors or supplier interface agreements are planned, they should be based on the Development Interface Agreement (DIA), as required by ISO 26262-8. Section 19.2 provides more information on this topic.

If planning for statistical evaluations, ISO/IEC 5469 for FuSa and AI includes a subchapter, "*AI system design with statistical evaluation*".

Agile Adaptation

Relevant agile adaptations for system design that have become popular involve developing part of it as MVP solutions and then improving. For instance, a company might aim to develop one MVP of the system in the next three months and then another belonging to the same system. Between the improvements of the MVPs, one should always consider the system level.

In addition, feedback from stakeholders is relevant to ensure the improvement of the most relevant functions after the first deployment.

Safety Plan Issues

Information from relevant stakeholders has become more important, so we should plan for communication with all the relevant stakeholders. This could also be part of the DIA as mentioned above. When developing a system, relevant standards are often more comprehensive at the system level as more standards are relevant for a system than fora product.

Chapter 15
Documentation, Information, and Work Products

Documentation serves as the backbone of a comprehensive safety plan, ensuring that all processes, requirements, and functions are clearly recorded and accessible. This chapter highlights the essential types of documentation—system, installation, user, and maintenance—and discusses how each contributes to a system's lifecycle from development through operation. Effective documentation must be accurate, user-focused, and kept up-to-date, supporting seamless communication and system usability across various stakeholder roles.

Objective

Documentation is a vital part of developing the safety plan and safety case. As the purpose of documentation is to provide information to people, parts of the documentation must be written in natural language and, when necessary, supported by comprehensible tables and diagrams. Three important requirements for all documentation are that it should be to the point, easy to understand, and up to date. Good documentation should always be able to answer three questions: how, why, and when.

Information

It is practical to split the documentation related to a high risk system into four main parts:

1. System documentation—what is done how and why?
2. Installation documentation—how to get the system or product up and running.
3. User documentation—how to use the system to solve the problems it is intended for.
4. Maintenance documentation—how to change or update the system in order to correct errors or to change the system's behaviour.

This topic is linked to the safety case chapter "Documentation and records" as part of the QMR. Several development projects refer to a "Documentation plan" that includes all relevant documents for the project. When improving an existing

© The Author(s) 2025
T. Myklebust et al., *The AI Act and The Agile Safety Plan*, SpringerBriefs in
Computer Science, https://doi.org/10.1007/978-3-031-80504-2_15

system, the documentation plan is often part of the change impact analysis (Myklebust & Stålhane, 2021). See Section 4.3 of *Functional Safety and Proof of Compliance* by Myklebust and Stålhane (2021, Springer) for a detailed discussion on this topic. See also Appendix A.

According to ISO 26262-1:2018 3.185 work product: "*documentation resulting from one or more associated requirements of ISO 26262.*

Note 1 to entry: The documentation can be in the form of a single document containing the complete information for the work product or a set of documents that together contain the complete information for the work product."

An example of a work product is an artefact used during a software development project, such as a requirements specification or class model diagram. As seen above, our definition of documentation includes all aspects of a work product.

The development process influences all types of documentation. Although the developers' main responsibility is software documentation, they will also need to participate in the development of other documentation. Development also influences the contents of these documents.

The four types of documentation are not independent and changes to one of them may introduce the need to change the two others. Some standards—e.g. ISO 26262—use the term "work product", which is documentation resulting from one or more associated requirements of ISO 26262. The documentation can be in the form of a single document containing the complete information for the work product or a set of documents that together contain the complete information for the work product.

Finally, a warning—some companies seriously believe that people not good enough for development can do documentation, which is some kind of low-level work. Choosing this path is company suicide. It will take some time, but the catastrophe is waiting in the near future.

Requirements

Several requirements in the AI Act are related to "System design". See Chap. 8 for more information.

It is important to link the documentation to the documentation users' needs, be it developers, maintainers, system users, or installers. Thus, while writing documentation, it is important to keep in mind what the user knows and what he wants to achieve. For software documentation it is important to keep the "why" in mind—why was it done like this, why did you choose that particular algorithm, and so on.

For user documentation and installation documentation, it is important to document error messages—what does each error message mean and what should you do to get around it. Note that the documentation requirements in the ISO 26262 series of standards focus mainly on content, and not on layout and appearance. The information need not be made available in physical documents. The documentation can take various forms and structures and tools can be used to generate documents automatically.

The IEC 61508 clearly describes that the objective of documentation is to specify the necessary information to be documented in order to ensure that:

- All phases of the overall E/E/PE system and software safety lifecycles can be effectively performed.
- The management of functional safety, verification, and the functional safety assessment activities can be effectively performed.

Agile Adaptation

If all documentation is produced when the product is handled over to the user(s), no agile adaptation is needed. There will be no changes before the user starts to use the product and any feedback or complaints are handled by the maintainers as in any other project.

When using the agile development process, however, we should develop all documentation in parallel with the code. This is also necessary in order to present the current product for the customers during the customer reviews.

Behaviour-driven development (BDD) (Abushama et al., 2021; Lenka et al., 2018; Patkar et al., 2021) is a development approach that encourages collaboration between various stakeholders, including developers, product owners, and users, to ensure that the desired behaviour of the system is well understood. Living documentation, which is closely related to BDD, refers to keeping the documentation of system behaviour up to date through automated acceptance tests. Unlike static documents, living documentation is dynamic and reflects the system's current state, providing a reliable reference for both the development and maintenance phases of a project. This living documentation helps ensure no regressions occur and supports knowledge transfer, particularly in large-scale projects. See also Sect. 4.2 "On living documents" in the book by Myklebust and Stålhane (2021).

Developing the system and the documentation in parallel will help us see the dependencies between the installation, development, and user documentation. However, this will add extra work to the project since we need to keep tabs on the documentation dependencies and may have to write new documentation when we change some code.

See also ISO/IEC/IEEE 26515:2018 "Systems and software engineering—Developing information for users in an agile environment" and Myklebust & Okoh (2022) regarding "Shippable documents".

Safety Plan Issues

The most important thing to remember is that we need to allocate time and personnel resources for documentation. We also need somebody to be responsible for keeping all the documentation updated and tracking dependencies. In addition, we need to document all decisions that will influence installation, maintenance, or use. This information will later serve as a basis for writing the final documentation.

Last but certainly not least, remember that documentation is not some kind of right-handed work. Yes, one of the authors is left-handed and proud of it.

Chapter 16
Human Aspects

Human considerations are central to the development of AI systems, especially in the context of agile safety planning. This chapter explores essential human aspects, such as situational awareness, controllability, and human oversight, which play a critical role in ensuring that high-risk AI systems operate safely and effectively. Through principles of human-centred design, the chapter also examines how interface design, agile development methods, and safety standards can support effective human–machine interaction. This understanding is essential for building AI systems that responsibly balance human involvement with automated processes in safety-critical environments.

Objective

Human aspects come into consideration in all phases in the development of the agile safety plan of AI-based systems. This chapter provides an overview of some human aspects that need to be considered from an AI and agile safety plan perspective. First, we introduce the concept of situational awareness. Next, we outline how the AI Act sets specific requirements to human oversight and how the term controllability relates to situational awareness. We also provide a brief overview of agile design principles for human–machine interfaces involving AI in high risk systems.

Information

In traditional human factors engineering, situational awareness is understood as a cognitive product made by input provided by the surroundings, as well as individual characteristics (Endsley, 1995). While AI systems in many cases are introduced to reduce workload enabling the human to step out of the loop, it often might come with the cost of reduced situational awareness when the human is required to be in the loop to handle safety-critical situations (Lee et al., 2017). Therefore, high risk AI systems need to be designed in a way that enables humans to achieve the sufficient level of situational awareness to fulfil the controllability function, i.e. the level of the ability to avoid harm by effectively managing, directing, or influencing the operation of a system. This will ensure smooth handovers from system to humans in the operation of the system. This requires careful attention to how functions are

© The Author(s) 2025
T. Myklebust et al., *The AI Act and The Agile Safety Plan*, SpringerBriefs in
Computer Science, https://doi.org/10.1007/978-3-031-80504-2_16

allocated between people and AI systems in the early design and development of these systems. Lee et al. (2017, p. 375) outline 15 principles of human-centred automation focusing on mental model principles, attention and perception principles, response selection and interaction principles, and organizational principles that will also be highly relevant when considering human-centred AI.

- Mental model principles will ensure that the purpose of the AI system, the operating domain, and the role of the human in the system is clearly defined, communicated, and understood.
- Attention and perception principles will ensure that the AI system is able to communicate in an understandable manner when it fails as well as to keep the human informed during task performance.
- The response selection and interaction principles underscore that design should ensure that accidental activation and deactivation do not occur and that handover from AI system to humans is timely, smooth, and coordinated ensuring situational awareness.
- The organizational principles relate to the need to pay careful attention to how the introduction of AI systems might require the training of new skills as well as consideration of the way new systems are developed, introduced, and implemented in organizational settings (Lee et al., 2017).

By focusing on these principles, a harmonization in the relationship between human and AI system might be facilitated.

While aspects relating to human aspects have not been explicitly treated in the safety case approach of EN 50129, Myklebust et al. (2025) suggest that human aspects and oversight (HAO) should be treated in a separate part in the safety case. This chapter corresponds directly to the HAO part in the safety case.

Requirements

The requirement of the AI Act Article 14 regarding human oversight is closely connected to the concept of situational awareness. The principle of human oversight means that humans should have control and decision-making power over important actions or processes, rather than relying solely on automated systems or algorithms. The AI Act Article 14 underscores that high risk AI systems should be developed and designed to enable humans to effectively oversee the use of AI systems. Human oversight should be ensured before a system is placed on the market or put into service. Sufficient human oversight is present when an individual given the role is able to:

- Fully understand both capacities and limitations of the AI system
- Able to detect eventual dysfunction
- To not suffer from automation bias manifested as an overreliance on the functioning of the system
- To decide when to not use a high risk AI system if the situation at hand requires it

On a general level one could claim that current requirements relating to human aspects in standards are weak and that human aspects are poorly described in functional safety standards. However, the concept of controllability in ISO 26262:2018

"Road vehicles- Functional Safety" points at the importance of considering it. Controllability is defined as the level of the ability to avoid harm. In the context of high risk systems, controllability is essential to ensure the safety of the systems in operation. Controllability ensures that systems do not take actions and make decisions that may have unforeseen consequences, and consequently controllability should be treated as a major aspect in the safety plan. Controllability is also one of the parameters that determine the ASIL. In conventional vehicles, the human driver accounts for controllability by being able to mitigate possible equipment malfunctions. Having a human present that should be able to intervene in a timely manner reduces the integrity requirements of a given system in these conventional vehicles. However, high risk AI systems challenge risk analyses that previously have accounted for controllability by having a human present that can react to unforeseen situations and equipment failures. When a car is fully autonomous, the responsibility of the human for managing unsafe equipment malfunctioning is removed, and the responsibility falls to the autonomy system. However, several safety-related AI systems will operate in combination with humans, for instance through autonomy functions such as Advanced Driver Assistance Systems (ADAS). These combinations of AI systems and humans operating in safety-critical environments require careful analysis of human–machine interfaces ensuring that they provide the sufficient situational awareness enabling humans to fulfil their controllability function.

In the context of controllability, ISO/IEC TS 8200:2024 "Information technology—Artificial Intelligence—Controllability of automated artificial intelligence systems" is also relevant to consider. In addition, ISO 5469 "Artificial intelligence—Functional Safety and AI systems" underscores that the level of autonomy of a system defines the control and intervention options of the human. If a human is added to a system to be a "supervisor" and intervene in critical situations, one should be aware that this does not necessarily reduce risks and can even introduce additional risks.

When developing the safety plan, the BSI PAS 1881:2022 *"Assuring the operational safety of automated vehicles—Specification"*, BSI Flex 1886:2023 *"System aspects for remote operation of vehicles—Guide"*, and BSI PAS 1884:2021 *"Safety operators in automated vehicle testing and trailing—Guide"* are worth considering. These standards bring in the importance of considering human factors in the operational safety assessments of automated vehicles, as well as in the system design of remote operation of vehicles. Two situations are particularly relevant in the design of AI system considering human aspects, namely "handover" and "intervention". A "handover" refers the "process by which the sustained dynamic driving task function transitions either from a human driver to an automated driving system or from an automated system to a human driver" (BSI PAS 1884:2021, p. 4). An "intervention", on the other hand, is framed as the "action or set of actions initiated by the safety operator to override automated operation and take control of the subject vehicle" (BSI PAS 1884:2021, p. 4). While the BSI standards relate to the automotive domain, also the IMO (International Maritime Organization) representing the maritime domain underscores the importance of human aspects by pointing at the importance of incorporating a human reliability analysis (HRA) when performing Formal Safety Assessments (IMO FSA, 2018).

Agile Adaptations

The importance of human–machine interfaces of high risk AI systems is underscored in the AI Act Article 14, pointing towards user-centred design as an important principle in the development of these systems. Following principles of user-centred design requires building knowledge into the specific user group as well as the context in which they operate in when performing the design process. Also, such a process should pay careful attention to how the human information processing process works and use this knowledge to guide the development of interfaces. Humans have a limited working memory and by paying attention to this in the design process one might ensure that working memory resources are not spent on unnecessary cognitive tasks (Lee et al., 2017). For instance, by ensuring that equipment is designed to provide input that does not entirely rely on the sense of sight, the load on working memory can be reduced. One possibility could be to provide tactile or haptic responses through buttons and interfaces, such that the sense of sight can be used for other critical tasks.

Several practices can facilitate development processes that consider human aspects. For instance, Behaviour-Driven Development (BDD) is a development method based on scenario descriptions, which might be combined with safety analysis methods to improve safety analysis and verification (Wang & Wagner, 2018). An example of such a safety analysis method is the Systems-Theoretic Process Analysis (STPA) that helps identify and prevent potential accidents by focusing on the overall system and how its components interact rather than just individual failures (Young & Leveson, 2014). Also, agile practices might be used in UX design, enabling quick changes in response to feedback from relevant stakeholders such as users, customers, safety experts, and regulatory authorities.

Safety Plan Issues

During system development, several aspects are relevant to consider.

- The requirements to assurance and certification will differ depending on whether the system is developed as an assistant system or as an autonomous system. An assistant system would in many cases be easier to certify. However, the handover situations between system and human need to be carefully designed, ensuring the sufficient level of situational awareness that enables interventions in a timely manner.
- If a human is part of the system to fulfil the controllability function, careful design of human–machine interfaces needs to be undertaken, considering mental model principles, attention principles, perception principles, response selection principles, interaction principles, and organizational principles.
- Most likely, new standards will be developed that specifically address the topic of human aspects. Our chapter provides an overview of the current state, but those interested in the topic should expect and pay attention to developments in the coming future.

Chapter 17
Level of Automation and Autonomy

Understanding the distinction between automation and autonomy is crucial as these two levels of system control shape how AI approaches, risk assessments, and requirements are structured. Automated systems operate on predefined instructions, performing tasks within set boundaries, while autonomous systems dynamically adapt and learn, evolving with their environments. This chapter explores these differences, along with the standards, regulations, and safety considerations that govern both automated and autonomous systems across various applications.

Objective

The EU regulation separates automatic systems from autonomous systems. Thus, it is important to understand the difference between the two types of systems since this will influence the AI approach, risk assessment, and system requirements in several ways.

Introduction

As a starter, keep in mind that the decisions made or actions taken by an automated system are based on predefined heuristics. On the other hand, an autonomous system "learns" and adapts to dynamic environments and evolves as the environment around it changes. When its environment changes, an autonomous system evolves and improves its behaviour over time, making it capable of handling more complex and unpredictable situations. UNECE Regulation 156 (REG. 30) states the importance of managing software updates for advanced systems. It mandates that manufacturers ensure that updates do not compromise safety or functionality, especially in autonomous systems. This regulation includes requirements to protect against unauthorized changes and to secure the update process, which is essential for maintaining the reliability of autonomous vehicles as they learn and adapt. The ISO 24089:2023 standard focuses on software update engineering for road vehicles but can be adapted to other systems and domains, offering guidelines to ensure safe and effective software updates. It outlines how organizations should plan, develop, and implement updates for vehicles and electronic control units (ECUs), emphasizing the importance of maintaining vehicle safety and cybersecurity throughout the

T. Myklebust et al., *The AI Act and The Agile Safety Plan*, SpringerBriefs in Computer Science, https://doi.org/10.1007/978-3-031-80504-2_17

process. The standard provides steps for verifying, validating, and approving software updates before deployment. It also covers how to manage software update campaigns, including communication with users, handling update dependencies, and ensuring the integrity of the software.

The following diagram, from SAE International (2021), shows their suggested levels of automation (Fig. 17.1):

Levels 0–2 are just regular driving, maybe with a driver support system for automatically dimming the headlight or turning on the windscreen wipers. Levels 4 and 5 imply automatic driving, while Level 3 is something between levels 2 and 4. Level 3 capabilities could include autonomous highway cruising and lane-keeping, allowing drivers to engage in other activities while the vehicle handles the task at hand. While the SAE levels cover different automated driving features, autonomous driving is beyond these levels. An autonomous car will have abilities beyond predefined automated driving features and as such be able to observe the environment and learn how to behave in new environments and situations.

Sheridan et al. (1978) original and ground-breaking work "Scale of Human–Machine Interaction" defines eight levels of automation:

1. Whole task done by human except for actual operation by machine
2. Human asks computer to suggest options and selects from the options

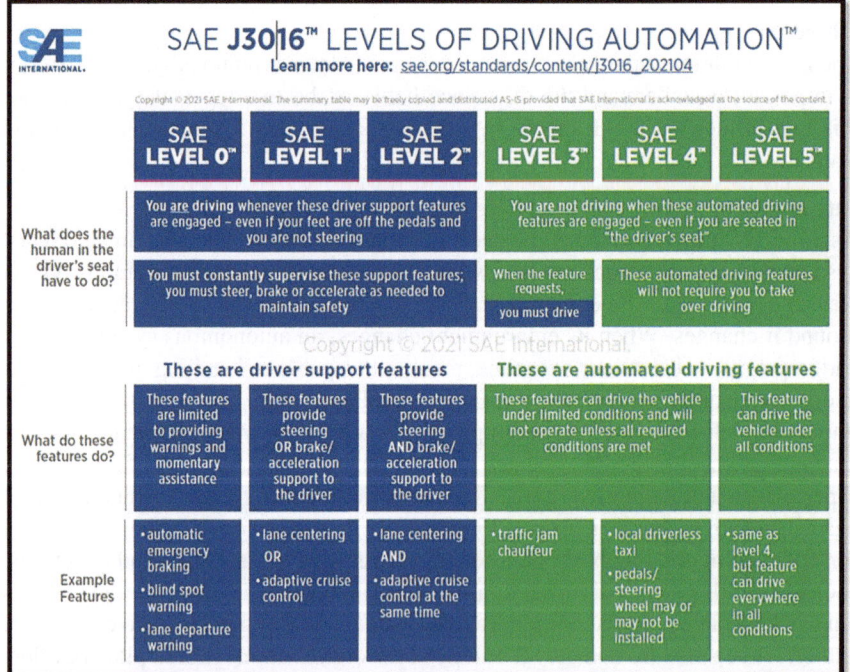

Fig. 17.1 Levels of autonomy. © SAE International from SAE J3016™ Taxonomy and Definitions for Terms Related to Driving Automation Systems for On-Road Motor Vehicles (2021-04-30), https://saemobilus.sae.org/content/J3016_202104/

Table 17.1 Levels of autonomy

Decision support	The crew is in direct command of ship operation and continuously supervises all operations. This level normally corresponds to "no autonomy"
Automatic	The operation follows a pre-programmed sequence and will request human intervention from either shore control Centre or the bridge if any unexpected events occur, or when the operation completes
Constrained autonomous	The ship can operate fully automatic in most situations and will call on human operators to intervene if problems cannot be solved within defined constraints. Shore control Centre or bridge personnel continuously supervise the operation and will take immediate control when requested by the system
Fully autonomous	The ship handles all situations by itself and will not have a shore control Centre or any bridge personnel at all

3. Computer suggests options to human
4. Computer suggests options and proposes one of them
5. Computer chooses an action and performs it if human approves
6. Computer chooses an action and performs it unless human disapproves
7. Computer chooses an action, performs it, and informs human
8. Computer does everything autonomously

We see that there are several similarities with SAE levels and level 8 even mentions autonomy. Last but not least, the following table, which was developed for maritime use, is instructive (Myhre et al., 2019) and the approach and results are generally applicable (Table 17.1).

Requirements

The EU's AI-Act "Whereas (12)" separates autonomy and automation as follows: *"Moreover, the definition should be based on key characteristics of AI systems that distinguish it from simpler traditional software systems or programming approaches and should not cover systems that are based on the rules defined solely by natural persons to automatically execute operations. A key characteristic of AI systems is their capability to infer."* See Chap. 8 for more information.

The main questions when deciding the level of automation or autonomy are:

• What is the users' level of knowledge and experience?
• How should the system be designed to ensure the situational awareness of operators?
• What are the consequences of a mishap?
• What are the planned environments and how well are they defined (ODD)?

Systems with SA levels 4 and 5 or automation levels 7 and 8 remove all control and responsibility from the users. Systems with SA levels 0–2 or automation levels 1–3 are support systems considered as "nice to have". In both cases, the highest level will relieve the user of the possibility to take control. See also Chap. 6 on human aspects—controllability. Some standards, e.g. UL 4600:2023, include requirements both to autonomous equipment—e.g. self-driving cars—and to automatic equipment—e.g. automatic doors.

Agile Adaptation

Changes to the planned system's environment and behaviour will influence the needed training data. To quote the EU AI act (2024): *"High-quality data sets for training, validation, and testing require the implementation of appropriate data governance and management practices. Data sets for training, validation and testing, including the labels, should be relevant, sufficiently representative, and to the best extent possible free of errors and complete in view of the system's intended purpose."*

The most important issue that separates automation and autonomy is the autonomy's need and requirements for high-quality training data.

Safety Plan Issues

When planning the project, the following things are important:

- Identify your customers—users, company marketing department, or others. For the developers, they are all "customers"
- Differentiation between automatic and autonomous systems
- Levels of automation
- Frequent communication in the project—what have I done, why have I done it, how it will influence another project member's decision, and so on.
- Regulatory/standards Focus on Safety and Updates; see Chap. 8
- Controllability; see Chap. 6

Chapter 18
A Process to Prepare Safety Cases

The chapters in the book have, until now, mainly focused on the different topics that should be included in the agile safety plan. However, as noted in the introduction, the work with the safety plan has a direct impact on *safety case* development. In this chapter, we first outline different types of safety cases and how an agile approach might facilitate an incremental development process. Next, we address how one should deal with related safety cases for subsystems, products, or modules. Lastly, we underscore the importance of preparing for improvements or modifications.

18.1 Preparing Safety Cases

Objective
The objective of establishing a process for developing safety cases by developers is to ensure that their developed systems have safety cases that provide arguments, supported by evidence, that the systems is safe for use in specific contexts. It aims to demonstrate that all potential hazards have been identified, assessed, and mitigated to an acceptable level, ensuring the system meets relevant safety standards and requirements. Which type of safety cases to be developed depends on the domain, project, and context.

Information
Several organizations, associations, and international standardization organizations have issued or are planning to issue requirements or guidelines related to the safety case or assurance case approach. While both safety case and assurance case are terms that are used in compliance contexts, an assurance case is a broader term than a safety case since it also includes cybersecurity cases.

The questions of whether a safety case should be developed and which type of safety case one should develop depend on the domain—e.g. the railway domain requires a safety case—and the relevant regions where the product or system shall

© The Author(s) 2025
T. Myklebust et al., *The AI Act and The Agile Safety Plan*, SpringerBriefs in
Computer Science, https://doi.org/10.1007/978-3-031-80504-2_18

be used. Both ISO 26262 and UL 4600 require a safety case, but these standards are not required to be used by law. In the Table 18.1, we have listed different safety cases in different projects.

A typical safety case refers to many reference documents. A typical reference list in a safety case includes 50–200 documents. Some safety cases have up to 400 references.

In addition, the safety standards have given titles to several documents: For example, the IEC 61508:2010 series mentions 82 documents with a title, 101 documents in the EN 5012X series, and 106 work products (documents) in the ISO 26262:2018 series. While a safety case normally consists of 100–300 pages, the referenced documents may consist of several thousand pages and sometimes more than 100,000 pages (see picture below) (Fig. 18.1).

This part of the safety plan has link to safety case chapter "Scope" which often is part of the "Introduction" of the safety case. In addition, the safety case refers to the last edition of the safety plan.

Table 18.1 Different assurance and safety cases	Assurance/safety case types
	Concept safety case
	Demonstration safety case
	Preliminary safety case
	Phase 4 EN 50126: "Specification of system requirements" safety case
	Modular safety case, product safety case
	Generic product safety case (GPSC)
	Generic application safety case (GASC)
	Specific application safety case (SASC)
	Supplier safety case
	Integrator safety case
	Site safety case
	Facility safety case
	Cross-acceptance safety case
	Modification safety case
	Dynamic assurance case
	Security case
	Cybersecurity case
	Operational design safety case
	System safety case
	"Top" safety case
	The prosecutor case
	The trust case
	Safety case for trial operations
	The safety case for the public

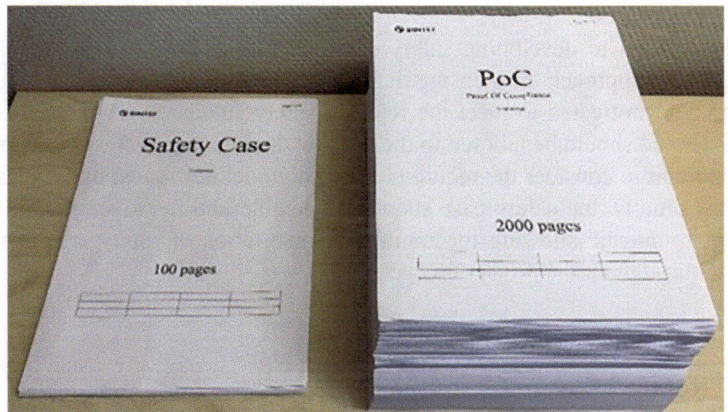

Fig. 18.1 Safety case and its references

Requirements

The AI Act does not have concrete requirements related to safety cases. The current edition of IEC 61508 does not include safety case requirements, but the next edition will include safety case information.

ISO 26262-1:2010 defines a safety case and includes requirements for a safety case in ISO 26262-2:2010, stating that the safety case shall be developed according to the safety plan and *"the safety case should progressively compile the work products that are generated during the safety lifecycle to support the safety argument."* ISO 26262-8:2010 includes a note related to supplier safety cases as part of distributed development. ISO 26262-10:2010 includes a short chapter, "5.2 Understanding of safety cases".

EN 50129 gives an extensive description of how safety cases should be structured into parts and relevant information about each part. Experience shows that there is a need for more guidelines, and that is why *The Agile Safety Case* book (Myklebust & Stålhane, 2018) was developed. Due to more modern and complex systems and AI, we have developed an improved structure based on EN 50129 that applies to the railway and other safety-critical domains (Myklebust et al., 2025).

Agile Adaptation

Adapting a safety case to an agile environment involves several key modifications that make the process more flexible and iterative. Firstly, the safety case should be developed incrementally, with safety arguments and evidence added continuously throughout the project rather than at the end. This approach enhances safety awareness and allows for early identification of potential issues. Secondly, documentation should be minimized and tailored to focus on essential safety elements, reducing unnecessary overhead. Finally, the safety case must be adaptable, allowing for changes in response to evolving requirements, thus ensuring that safety is maintained even as the system develops (Myklebust & Stålhane, 2021).

Safety Plan Issues

The plan related to developing safety cases should start by establishing a clear objective. The approach must ensure that all potential hazards have been identified, assessed, and mitigated to meet the relevant safety standards. The type of safety case developed should be tailored to the specific domain and context of the project. It is important to consider the requirements and guidelines issued by various organizations. Finally, the safety case should be flexible and iterative, particularly in agile environments, allowing for continuous integration of safety arguments and evidence throughout the project lifecycle.

18.2   Related Safety Cases

Objective

The objective of this safety plan is to ensure that all relevant subsystems, products, modules, items, or equipment upon which the system under consideration depends are identified and documented in the related safety case. Additionally, the objective is to establish clear dependencies between safety cases, ensuring that the safety case for a system appropriately references any necessary safety cases from subsystems, generic products, or applications.

Information

A system normally consists of several modules and products.

> Related safety cases of any system are subsystems, products, items, or equipment on which the system under consideration depends.

Other names are hierarchical or modular safety cases on which the systems safety case depends (The Agile Safety Case book Sect. 10.1 "Introduction to related safety cases" in Myklebust and Stålhane (2018)). SEooC as we have mentioned in Sect. 19.2 should be supplied with a safety case.

Requirements

The AI Act has no concrete requirements related to safety cases. Only EN 50129 for the railway domain includes concrete requirements for related safety cases. Below, we have adapted these requirements that should apply to any safety domain:

This part shall contain references to the safety cases of any system, subsystems, Safety Elements out of Context (SEooCs), or products on which the system under consideration depends.

It shall also demonstrate that all the safety-related application conditions specified in the Safety

Cases have been either:

- Fulfilled in the system under consideration
- Carried forward as safety-related application conditions

When the safety case includes other Generic Product or Application Safety Cases, the version of the related products/applications shall be reported here.

Agile Adaptations

Companies that develop modular systems, SEooC, products, or similar should have an agile approach that can be synchronized. In addition, the adaptations mentioned above apply.

Safety Plan Issues

The safety plan should ensure that all subsystems, products, modules, and products the system relies on are clearly identified and documented in the relevant safety case. It will also establish clear links between the system's safety case and any related cases for subsystems or products, ensuring consistency and avoiding duplicate assessments. SEooCs should have their own safety case to ensure safe integration into the overall system.

The plan should ensure that it is verified that all safety-related application conditions are either fulfilled in the current system or carried forward for future reference. It will also document the exact versions of any referenced generic product or application safety cases.

18.3 Planning for Modifications

Objective

The agile safety plan must include plan measures that ensure that any relevant AI and safety changes to the system that could significantly alter its intended purpose, performance, or risk profile are carefully evaluated and managed. This process is crucial for maintaining the AI system's compliance with regulatory requirements and relevant AI and FuSa standards. The goal is to proactively identify and mitigate potential new risks introduced by such modifications, thereby ensuring the continued safe operation of the AI system in its intended environment. This *part of the safety plan* should be evaluated together with the deployment/release plan.

Information

Change Impact Analysis (CIA) is a crucial process, as described in Sect. 4.3 ('Change Impact Analysis Report') of Functional Safety and Proof of Compliance by Myklebust and Stålhane (2021), for assessing how changes, updates, upgrades, or modifications to a software system might impact other parts of the system or its overall safety and functionality. This analysis is particularly important in safety-critical systems, where any change could have significant consequences.

Whenever a change or modification is proposed to a software system, it is essential to analyse its potential effects on the entire system. This ensures that the change does not inadvertently introduce new risks. The CIA helps understand the potential consequences of a change by identifying which parts of the system could be affected and ensuring that the necessary precautions are taken to maintain safety and performance. As software evolves over time, CIA ensures that each new version is thoroughly examined for potential impacts on the system's safety and functionality. Regression testing is performed before releasing a new software version to ensure that existing features still work as expected after the change.

Tool support is essential when modifying safety-critical software. It ensures that changes are systematically tracked, analysed, and verified, thereby minimizing the risk of introducing errors that could compromise safety. For more information about the use of tools, see Chap. 11.

Requirements

The AI Act defines "substantial modification"; see Appendix C. The Act also requires to

- Have "*a strategy for regulatory compliance, including compliance with conformity assessment procedures and procedures for the management of modifications to the high risk AI system*".
- Providers should if "*they make a substantial modification to a high risk AI system that has already been placed on the market or has already been put into service in such a way that it remains a high risk AI system pursuant to Article 6*".
- High risk AI systems that have already been subject to a conformity assessment procedure shall undergo a new change impact analysis.
- Include "*conformity assessment procedure in the event of a substantial modification, regardless of whether the modified system is intended to be further distributed or continues to be used by the current deployer*".

See also Chap. 8.

Regarding "Software update" and requirements in UNECE 156 (REG. 30) and ISO 24089:2023, see Chap. 17.

Modification is not defined in IEC 61508-4:2010 and EN 50129:2018 but in ISO 26262-1:2018 as "*3.91 Modification. Creation of a new item from an existing item*".

The safety standards should be improved in future editions, related to changes and modifications. One of the authors has been involved in parts of this improvement of IEC 61508-3 for software related to regression testing when performing changes.

IEC 61508 has a safety phase 15 named "Overall modification and retrofit". The safety standards require an impact analysis before modifications are started.

For further information, see also ISO/IEC 5469:2024 Table A.8 Interpretation of modification and IEC 61508-3:2010, Table A.8 Modification.

Agile Adaptation

A "Predetermined Change Control Plan" (PCCP) is a structured approach that allows for specific, planned changes to a product's software or hardware to be made in a planned and agile manner. For an agile safety plan, you often can anticipate and manage modifications to your system without needing a full re-approval each time, as long as the changes align with the predefined guidelines and maintain the safety and effectiveness of the product/system.

Safety Plan Issues

The safety plan should include a robust process for evaluating and managing changes and modifications that could significantly impact the system's purpose, performance, or risk profile to ensure ongoing compliance with regulatory requirements and relevant AI and functional safety standards. CIA is critical for identifying and mitigating potential risks introduced by modifications, ensuring that the system continues to operate safely and effectively. The plan should also integrate tool support to track, analyse, and verify changes systematically, with regression testing conducted to confirm that existing features remain unaffected by updates. Additionally, the plan must align with regulatory requirements, such as those outlined in the AI Act, and safety standards like IEC 61508, which mandate a thorough impact analysis before any modifications are implemented.

When having subcontractors and Development Interface Agreement (DIA) is relevant, all these issues and aspects should be included as part of the contract. For more information, see Chap. 19.

Chapter 19
Procurement and Subcontractors

This chapter covers relevant topics related to procurement and subcontractors. First, we outline which aspects developers should consider when buying components to be used as parts of the system being developed. These aspects cover how to organize the procurement process by clearly defining roles and responsibilities, as well as how to ensure access and insights into relevant certificates and documentation accompanying the components. Next, we outline how subcontracting is an important business-related consideration that needs to be addressed in several development projects.

Relevant Topics for Procurement and Subcontracts
Several functional safety standards have evolved based on IEC 61508, each adding industry-specific requirements. Rapid technological advancements can outpace these standards, leading to unguided interpretation and potentially obsolete designs. Promoting cross-domain reuse of safety resources helps address this by allowing advanced industries to support others (Okoh & Myklebust, 2024a, 2024b). However, a clear framework for such exchanges is essential to prevent confusion and negative impact on safety outcomes.

When purchasing products or including products from subcontractors, it is important to understand how integration works. This is where an Application Programming Interface (API) is used. An API is a set of instructions or guidelines that inform different software components how to work together. A good API simplifies software development by giving developers the tools they need. APIs must offer comprehensive documentation, robust error handling, and extensive testing tools to ensure reliability and correctness. Real-time performance management and built-in security features are essential to meet stringent safety and timing requirements.

In addition to APIs, developers often work with Software Development Kits (SDK) and Accessory Development Kits (ADK), which serve slightly different purposes but are equally important.

© The Author(s) 2025
T. Myklebust et al., *The AI Act and The Agile Safety Plan*, SpringerBriefs in Computer Science, https://doi.org/10.1007/978-3-031-80504-2_19

An SDK is a toolbox for developers. It includes all the tools, libraries, and resources they need to create software for a specific item or component. An ADK is similar to an SDK but is specifically designed to create add-ons or accessories for existing devices. For instance, if a company makes a camera, they might provide an ADK to help developers create accessories that work seamlessly with that camera, like a remote control or a special lens. The ADK ensures the accessories will work properly with the main device. "Interface as a Service" has also become popular and refers to providing a cloud-based platform or service that allows developers to interact with AI models or systems through predefined interfaces such as APIs or microservices.

19.1   Procurement

Objective

The objective of this part of the safety plan is to ensure that all purchased components meet the relevant AI and safety requirements, thus reducing risks during integration and operation. The plan guides procurement by specifying necessary safety documentation and certificates, ensuring that supplied components align with relevant safety standards. It also aims to streamline approvals, minimize delays, and ensure timely access to critical safety information for engineers.

Information

When purchasing software, buyers should ensure that the supplier's team has clear roles and responsibilities to maintain safety assessments of AI. Buyers should check that the software development process follows a structured lifecycle with thorough planning, documentation, and quality control. In addition, they should assess the robustness of testing and verification procedures to ensure that the software meets safety and functionality requirements. Compatibility with existing systems and the ability to avoid buyer's regret through careful goal alignment and risk assessment are also key considerations. This safety plan chapter links to a similar chapter in the safety case.

Requirements

The EU's AI-Act "Whereas" no. 143 states: "*In order to address the specific needs of SMEs, including start-ups, the Commission should provide standardised templates for the areas covered by this Regulation, upon request of the Board. Additionally, the Commission should complement Member States' efforts by providing a single information platform with easy-to-use information with regards to this Regulation for all providers and deployers, by organising appropriate communication campaigns to raise awareness about the obligations arising from this Regulation, and by evaluating and promoting the convergence of best practices in public procurement procedures in relation to AI systems*".

Article 25 "Responsibilities along the AI value chain" should also be considered. Regarding Article 26 "Obligations of deployers of high risk AI systems", see Chap. 8.

ISO 9001:2015 (STD23) includes requirements in 8.4 Control of externally provided processes, products, and services and guidelines in A.8 Control of externally provided processes, products, and services. The IEC 61508 committee is developing a new TR, IEC 61508-6-1, *"Treatment of hardware or software developed to ISO 26262"*, which hopefully will be issued in 2025 (Okoh & Myklebust, 2024a, 2024b).

Safety standards emphasize the importance of clear responsibilities and role independence within supplier teams to ensure objective software safety assessments. Suppliers are required to document the qualifications and ongoing training of their personnel to maintain competence. The development process must follow a structured approach, including thorough planning, documentation, and quality control. Robust testing and verification procedures are essential to ensure that the software meets the specified requirements and complies with safety and integrity standards.

The 2010 edition of IEC 61508 introduced the concept safety manual. The purpose of a safety manual for a compliant item, with e.g. IEC 61508, is to document all information relating to the item according to the definition in IEC 61508-4:2010. This is required to enable the integration of the compliant item into a safety-related system, a subsystem, or an element to comply with the requirements of this standard. The safety manual is not mentioned in the CENELEC EN 5012x standards. However, it is still important, especially at the Generic Product (GP) level, since designers and integrators of products, equipment, or systems need the information presented in the safety manual to ensure that the integration can be performed without compromising safety. Requirements for the content of the safety manuals are presented both in IEC 61508-2:2010—Hardware part of the requirements—and in IEC 61508-3:2010—Software part of the requirements.

ISO 26262 introduced the term "Safety Elements out of Context" (SEooC); see ISO 26262-10:2018, clause 9. A SEooC is a safety-related element that is not developed for a specific item—i.e. it is not developed in the context of a particular vehicle type. It must, however, be developed according to the ISO 26262 standard. As an example, consider a generic brake system with assumed safety requirements to be integrated into different OEM (Original Equipment Manufacturer) systems.

The ASIL capability of a SEooC designates its ability to comply with assumed safety requirements assigned to a given ASIL. Consequently, it defines the requirements of the ISO 26262 series of standards that are applied to the development of this SEooC. See also Sect. 18.2.

Agile Adaptation
It is important to incorporate agile adaptations that allow for iterative assessment and integration of the purchased products. Frequent sprint reviews, where AI and safety engineers are involved, should include evaluations of safety products to

ensure they meet evolving project requirements and regulatory standards. Collaboration with suppliers should be frequent, with feedback loops established to promptly address any deficiencies or updates. By maintaining flexibility and fostering an adaptive procurement strategy, teams can better align the safety products with the project's dynamic needs while ensuring compliance and mitigating risks.

Safety Plan Issues
The safety plan's main issue is ensuring that all purchased components meet safety requirements. The plan emphasizes the importance of a structured software development process, including robust testing and verification procedures, to ensure compliance with safety standards. Agile adaptations are also important, enabling iterative assessment and integration of safety products to align with evolving project needs and regulatory standards. Finally, compatibility with existing systems and cross-domain reuse of safety resources are crucial for mitigating risks and streamlining the integration process.

19.2   Subcontractor Management Arrangements

Objective
This part of the safety plan aims to define the responsibilities between customers and subcontractors during distributed developments. It ensures that safety planning by both parties aligns with the agreed-upon responsibilities, helping to manage interactions, dependencies, and the exchange of work products effectively throughout the development process.

Information
Sub-contracting is common in the automotive domain. Subcontractor management arrangements involve overseeing the work of companies hired to do specific tasks or supply parts. It is about ensuring these subcontractors meet deadlines, stick to the budget, and deliver quality work. This involves clear communication, setting expectations, and sometimes checking their work to ensure everything aligns with the project's goals. Good management of subcontractors helps avoid delays and ensures a successful final product. See also the section above regarding procurement.

Original Equipment Manufacturers (OEM) create the final product, like a car or a computer, sold under their brand. Companies that supply parts to OEMs are called Tier suppliers. Tier 1 suppliers provide major components directly to the OEM, while Tier 2 suppliers provide parts to Tier 1 suppliers. Tier 3 companies are further down the chain, supplying raw materials or essential components that Tier 2 suppliers use to make more complex parts. Even though Tier 3 companies are at the beginning of the supply chain, their effective management is crucial. The quality and availability of the materials and components they provide directly impact the entire manufacturing process and, ultimately, the final product's performance and reliability. Therefore, a well-coordinated and efficient supply chain, starting with Tier 3 suppliers, is essential for producing high-quality end products that meet customer expectations.

Table 19.1 Development interface agreement topics and new relevant AI topics

Relevant topics in a DIA are (ISO 26262-8:2018):	Weak parts and AI topics that should be added as part of the DIA
• Pre-qualifications and qualifications • Acceptance of conditions • Capability issues and safety goals • Compliance issues • Iterative evaluations • Supplier safety plan and HARA (see Sect. 5.2) • Proven in use • Development lifecycle issues • Design issues and integration issues • Tests, verifications, and validations	• SRACs should be reported early to the integrator • SRACs should be clearly stated • AI act compliance • Scope of AI services • Data management • Evolvement of the AI system • Modifications • Future proofing of the AI system

This safety plan chapter links to a similar chapter in the safety case. Subcontractor management arrangements are linked to the "system/sub-system/equipment design" chapter of the SMR (Myklebust et al., 2025).

Requirements

See Sect. 19.2. IEC 61508 is weak regarding distributed development and contracts. However, both IEC 61508-2 and IEC 61508-3 include requirements for a safety manual, which is an important delivery from the subcontractor to the integrator.

The Development Interface Agreement (DIA) in the automotive safety standard ISO 26262 is a document somewhat similar to the safety manual. The safety planning is documented, and the plan includes a reference to the development interface agreements (ISO 26262-8:2018, Clause 5). The DIA defines the interfaces with the safety plans of the other stakeholders, often a subcontractor. Annex B, "Development Interface Agreement example", presents an example of a DIA. In the Table 19.1 we have added relevant topics when AI is part of the contract.

Agile Adaptation

The Agile Manifesto 2001 states, *"Customer collaboration over contract negotiation"*. As part of the SafeScrum (Hanssen et al. 2018), we suggested changing this to:

> Customer collaboration AND contract negotiation

With the increased complexity and additional topics related to AI this has strengthened our view. It is possible to establish an agile contract. The Norwegian Agency for Public Management and eGovernment has issued guidelines for agile contracts. For further information, see also DFØ (2023). This document outlines a detailed Agile Software Development Agreement. The agreement governs software delivery using an agile development method and includes provisions on roles, responsibilities, communication, testing, handover, warranties, and more.

Safety Plan Issues

Early in the project, one should consider the AI aspects listed in the table above. If relevant, one should consider establishing an agile contract. Integrators should require that a safety manual, according to IEC 61508, is part of the delivery. Companies working in other domains than automotive should consider including a DIA as part of their contracts.

Appendices

Appendix A: Documents that Are Referenced in the Agile Safety Plan and the Agile Safety Case

"Tell me and I forget, teach me and I may remember, involve me and I learn."
— Attributed to *Benjamin Franklin*

Introduction

This chapter includes an overview of relevant named documents in our projects and especially named documents and work products (automotive) in functional safety standards.

In this overview, we have limited the evaluated safety standards to the

- Generic safety standard IEC 61508 series
- Automotive safety standard ISO 26262 series
- Railway standard series EN 5012X and EN 50716:2023

Relevant Documents Not Mentioned in the Main Safety Standards

The safety standards have different approaches to documentation. While the railway standards use "documents", the automotive standard uses "work products". Other standards, such as the generic IEC 61508 series, are not specific but mention the topic in Appendix A of IEC 61508-1:2010.

Documents not mentioned in these three standard series but often used by several manufacturers are (Table A.1):

© The Author(s) 2025
T. Myklebust et al., *The AI Act and The Agile Safety Plan*, SpringerBriefs in
Computer Science, https://doi.org/10.1007/978-3-031-80504-2

Table A.1 Documents not mentioned in functional safety standards

Documents	Safety plan chapters	Relevant standards and guidelines
1. Safety T&M to be used according to AI and safety standards development projects.	9 Testing	Some functional safety standards include relevant T&M that should be performed in the development. In our experience, a good approach is to plan for this and establish a separate document for this work • Appendix *"Applicability of IEC 61508-3 to AI technology elements"* in ISO/IEC TR 5469:2024 (STD33) • IEC 61508-2:2010 Appendices A and B "…Techniques and measures. …" • IEC 61508-3:2010 Appendix B "…Techniques and measures…" Appendix B "Detailed tables" • IEC 61508-7:2010 "Overview of techniques and measures" • EN 50716:2023. Appendix D (informative) Bibliography of techniques • ISO 26262 series (named methods and integrated in the standard series, thus not in an Appendix) • Proof of compliance book (Myklebust et al., 2021) Chapter 4.5 "Safety Techniques and measures: Software"
2. FAT, SAT, DAT, SIT, and CAT. FAT and SAT are mentioned in several standards	9 Testing	Several well-known tests are still very important and described in the standards listed below. These are Factory Acceptance Test (FAT), Site Acceptance Test (SAT), Development Acceptance Test (DAT), Site Integration Test (SIT), and Customer/Compliance Acceptance test (CAT) • IEC 61511:2016 series • IEC TR 61511-4:2020 • IEC 62381:2012 includes requirements for SIT • IEC 62708:2015 defines specific documents and their basic content required for electrical and instrumentation projects in the process industry. It specifies the document kind name and the mandatory content of the document kind
3. ODD/OEDR description	3 ODD	In the last 5–10 years, description of ODD has received much attention due to especially autonomous vehicles. • SAE J3016 International, 2021 • SAE AVSC00002202004:2020 AVSC Best Practice for Describing an Operational Design Domain (ODD): Conceptual Framework and Lexicon • ISO TS 23860:2022 Ships and marine technology—Vocabulary related to autonomous ship systems uses "Operational envelope" and not ODD (Operational Design Domain) and presents their arguments for using another name in B.3 • ISO 34503:2023 Road Vehicles—Road Vehicles—Test scenarios for automated driving systems—Specification for operational design domain • BSI PAS 1883:2020 Operational Design Domain (ODD) taxonomy for an automated driving system (ADS)—Specification • BSI PAS 1884 2021. Safety operators in automated vehicle testing and trialling—Guide

(continued)

Table A.1 (continued)

Documents	Safety plan chapters	Relevant standards and guidelines
4. Site assessment report (SAR)	3 ODD	Often used as part of trial operations We also include information regarding the Safety Assessment Report (SAR) in Chap. 18 • ISO 22737:2021 Intelligent transport systems—Low-speed automated driving (LSAD) systems for predefined routes—Performance requirements, system requirements and performance test procedures • ISO 11270:2014 Intelligent transport systems—Lane keeping assistance systems (LKAS)—Performance requirements and test procedures • UNECE reg 157 ALKS level 3. ALKS: Automatic Lane Keeping System
5. Operational risk assessment	12	Often used as part of trial operations. This has similarities with HazOp • IEC 61882:2016 Hazard and operability studies (HAZOP studies)—Application guide • SCSC Data guide 2024. Appendix F HAZOP Guidewords—Detail (Informative)
6. Emergency and response plan	3 ConOps	Often used as part of trial operations • BSI PAS 1881:2022 Assuring the operational safety of automated vehicles—Specification
7. SRAC document	12.5 SRAC	A pragmatic approach used by the railway domain • F. Bitsch, U. Feucht, and H. Gough. SRAC. Safety-Related Application Conditions—A Balance between Safety Relevance and Handicaps for Applications. SafeComp 2009 Proceedings of the 28th International Conference on Computer Safety, Reliability, and Security Pages 32–45 • The Agile Safety Case book chapter 9.5 "SRAC" (Myklebust & Stålhane, 2018) • UNECE DCAS. Chap. 5.6 Driver Information Materials. This clause requires similar information
8. Common cause report	12 Hazards and risks	Common cause is often a challenge and as a result, a report evaluating common cause issues and challenges is issued as part of the project • NOROG 070 rev.5 (2022) • IEC 61508:2010 series • EN 50126-2:2017 (STD9) • Nuclear Regulatory Commission. (n.d./2015). Transmittal of Research Information Letter RIL-1101: Technical basis to review hazard analysis of digital safety systems

Planning Documents

In this part, we have listed planning documents that are mentioned in these standards:

- Generic safety standard IEC 61508 series
- Automotive safety standard ISO 26262 series
- Railway standard series EN 5012X and EN 50716:2023
- SCSC Data guide 2024

Understanding other relevant plans is crucial for ensuring comprehensive safety management as part of an agile safety plan. Agile projects often require flexibility and rapid responses to change, making it essential to align with various documents such as safety validation, verification, and maintenance plans. By considering these other plans, stakeholders can ensure that safety measures are consistently applied across all stages of the project lifecycle, helping to avoid gaps in safety procedures and supporting a more integrated approach.

Planning documents (as they are named in the standards):

1 Plan (overall operation and maintenance)
2 Plan (overall operation and maintenance)
3 Plan (overall safety validation)
4 Plan (overall installation);
5 Plan (overall commissioning)
6 Data safety management plan (SCSC Guide)
7 Plan (overall decommissioning or disposal);
8 Plan (safety);
9 Plan (verification);
10 Plan (functional safety assessment);
11 Plan (E/E/PE system safety validation)
12 Plan (E/E/PE system safety);
13 Plan (E/E/PE system verification);
14 Plan (E/E/PE system functional safety assessment);
15 Plan (software safety validation)
16 Plan (software safety);
17 Plan (software verification);
18 Plan (software functional safety assessment);
19 Software Quality Assurance Plan
20 Software Configuration Management Plan
21 Software Verification Plan
22 Software Validation Plan
23 Application Preparation Plan
24 Software Release and Deployment Plan
25 Software Maintenance Plan
26 Software Assessment Plan
27 Suppliers' safety plan
28 Configuration management plan

29 Change management plan
30 "Impact analysis" and "change request plan"
31 Verification plan
32 Documentation management plan
33 Hardware element evaluation plan
34 Hardware component test plan

Relevant Documents to Be Referenced by the Safety Case

In this part, we have listed relevant documents that are mentioned in these standards:

- Generic safety standard IEC 61508 series
- Automotive safety standard ISO 26262 series
- Railway standard series EN 5012X and EN 50716:2023
- SCSC Data Guide 2024

As part of an agile safety plan, it is essential to be aware of relevant documents that will be referenced in the safety case to ensure alignment and coherence across all safety aspects. These documents, such as verification plans, safety validation reports, and risk assessments, provide critical context and support for the arguments made within the safety case. By understanding these referenced documents, stakeholders can ensure that the agile safety plan remains robust, comprehensive, and compliant with relevant safety standards, helping to establish a strong foundation for the safety case.

1. Analysis of safety goal violations due to random hardware failures
2. Analysis of the effectiveness of the architecture of the item to cope with the random hardware failures
3. Application Architecture and Design
4. Application Data/Algorithms Verification Report
5. Application Preparation Verification Report
6. Application Release Notes (software)
7. Application Requirements Specification
8. Application Test Report
9. Application Test Specification
10. Base vehicle manufacturer or supplier guideline
11. Calibration data
12. Calibration Data Specification
13. Change report
14. Change request
15. Configuration data
16. Configuration Data Specification
17. Confirmation measure reports
18. Database or report (Hazard log)
19. Data safety management plan (SCSC Guide)

20. Definition of system
21. Delivery sheet or release note
22. Dependent failure analysis report
23. Description and report (hazard and risk analysis)
24. Description (E/E/PE system architecture design, comprising: hardware architecture and software architecture)
25. Description (functional safety concept)
26. Description (hardware architecture design)
27. Description (overall concept)
28. Description (overall safety requirements allocation)
29. Description (overall scope definition)
30. Description (software architecture design)
31. Description (software system design)
32. Description of candidate for proven in use argument
33. Description of interfaces
34. Documentation of the software development environment
35. Embedded software
36. Evidence of competence management
37. Evidence of quality management system
38. Hardware design specification (including test and evaluation criteria)
39. Hardware design verification report
40. Hardware element evaluation report for hardware elements
41. Hardware integration and verification report
42. Hardware integration and verification specification
43. Hardware modules
44. Hardware safety analysis report
45. Hardware safety requirements specification (including test and qualification criteria)
46. Hardware safety requirements verification report
47. Hardware-software interface (HSI) specification
48. Hardware-software interface specification (refined)
49. Hazard log
50. Identified safety anomaly reports
51. Impact analysis at element level
52. Impact analysis at the item level
53. Instruction (development tools)
54. Instruction (development tools and coding manual)
55. Instruction (E/E/PE system modification procedures)
56. Instruction (operation and maintenance)
57. Instruction (software modification procedures)
58. Instruction (user)
59. Integration and test report
60. Integration and test strategy
61. List (source code)
62. Log (E/E/PE system modification)

63. Log (overall decommissioning or disposal)
64. Log (overall modification and retrofit)
65. Log (overall operation and maintenance)
66. Modification procedures
67. Organization-specific rules and processes for functional safety
68. Overall Software Test Report
69. Overall Software Test Specification
70. Proven in use analysis reports
71. Release for production report
72. Report (code review)
73. Report (deployment)
74. Report (E/E/PE system functional safety assessment)
75. Report (E/E/PE system modification impact analysis)
76. Report (E/E/PE system safety validation)
77. Report (E/E/PE system verification)
78. Report (functional safety assessment)
79. Report (hardware modules tests)
80. Report (overall commissioning)
81. Report (overall decommissioning or disposal impact analysis)
82. Report (overall installation)
83. Report (overall modification and retrofit impact analysis)
84. Report (overall safety validation)
85. Report (programmable electronic and other hardware integration tests)
86. Report (programmable electronic hardware and software integration tests)
87. Report (release)
88. Report (software architecture integration tests)
89. Report (software deployment)
90. Report (software module integration tests)
91. Report (software module tests)
92. Report (software modification impact analysis)
93. Report (software release)
94. Report (software safety validation)
95. Report (software system integration tests)
96. Report (user manual)
97. Safety analysis report
98. Safety case
99. Safety manual for compliant items
100. Safety plan
101. Safety rationale
102. Safety validation report
103. Safety validation specification including safety validation environment description
104. Software Architecture and Design Verification Report
105. Software Architecture Specification
106. Software assessment report

107. Software Change Records
108. Software component documentation
109. Software Component Design Specification
110. Software Component Design Verification Report
111. Software Component Qualification Report
112. Software Component Qualification Verification Report
113. Software Component Test Report
114. Software Component Test Specification
115. Software deployment manual
116. Software Design Specification
117. Software Integration Test Report
118. Software Integration Test Specification
119. Software Integration Verification Report
120. Software Maintenance Records
121. Software Maintenance Verification Report
122. Software planning verification report
123. Software Quality Assurance Verification Report
124. Software Requirements Specification
125. Software Requirements Verification Report
126. Software safety requirement specification
127. Software Source Code and Supporting Documentation
128. Software Source Code Verification Report
129. Software system integration tests specification
130. Specification (E/E/PE system safety requirements, comprising: E/E/PE system safety functions requirements and E/E/PE system safety integrity requirements)
131. Specification (hardware architecture integration tests)
132. Specification (hardware module design)
133. Specification (hardware module tests)
134. Specification (integration tests of programmable electronic and non-programmable electronic hardware)
135. Specification (overall safety requirements, comprising: overall safety functions requirements and overall safety integrity requirements)
136. Specification (programmable electronic hardware and software integration tests)
137. Specification (programmable electronic integration tests)
138. Specification (software architecture integration tests)
139. Specification (software module design)
140. Specification (software module tests)
141. Specification (software safety requirements, comprising: software safety functions requirements and software safety integrity requirements)
142. Supplier selection report
143. Supply agreement
144. System architectural design specification
145. Technical safety concept

146. Technical safety requirements specification
147. Tools Validation Report
148. Validation of tools
149. Verification report
150. Verification report for system architectural design, the hardware-software interface (HIS) specification, the specification of requirements for production, operation, service and decommissioning, and the technical safety

Appendix B: AI Act Technical Documentation and Links to Safety Plan, Safety Case, and Named Documents

AI Act Appendix IV Technical Documentation Referred to in Article 11(1)

The technical documentation referred to in Article 11(1) shall contain at least the following information, as applicable to the relevant AI system:

AI Act requirements	Link to A: Safety plan chapters B: Safety case chapters C: Named Safety case references
1. A general description of the AI system including: (a) • Its intended purpose • The name of the provider • The version of the system reflecting its relation to previous versions	A: ConOps B: ConOps C: User manual, Datasheet (Appendix A), Release notes (PoC book chapter 8.3.2 "Release notes") Bullet three: The system's version indicates how it has evolved or improved compared to earlier versions
(b) How the AI system interacts or can be used to interact with hardware or software, including other AI systems, which are not part of the AI system itself, where applicable	A: Chapter 14 B: *The Agile Safety Case* in 2018 (Myklebust & Stålhane, 2018) and AI safety report (Myklebust et al., 2025) C: User manual
(c) The versions of relevant software or firmware and any requirement related to version update	A: DoS B: DoS C: Impact analysis, User manual, Datasheet (Appendix A), Release notes (PoC book chapter 8.3.2 "Release notes")
(d) The description of all forms in which the AI system is placed on the market or put into service (e.g. software package embedded into hardware, downloadable, API, etc.)	A: DoS, Subcontractor information B: DoS, Subcontractor information, and AI safety report (Myklebust et al., 2025) C: User manual

AI Act requirements	Link to A: Safety plan chapters B: Safety case chapters C: Named Safety case references
(e) The description of hardware on which the AI system is intended to run	A: DoS B: DoS C: Dos as a separate document
(f) Where the AI system is a component of products, photographs, or illustrations showing external features, marking and internal layout of those products	A: DoS, Related safety case B: DoS, Related safety case (Myklebust et al., 2018) C: Related safety cases are references of the main system safety case
(g) a basic description of the user-interface provided to the deployer;	A: DoS, Related safety case B: DoS, Related safety case C: Interface report
(h) Instructions of use for the deployer and a basic description of the user interface provided to the deployer where applicable	A: DoS B: DoS, System architecture description (Myklebust et al., 2018) and AI safety report (Myklebust et al., 2025). C: User manual and safety manual
(i) instructions for use for the deployer, and a basic description of the user-interface provided to the deployer, where applicable	A: DoS B: DoS C: User manual
2. A detailed description of the elements of the AI system and of the process for its development, including: (a) The methods and steps performed for the development of the AI system, including, where relevant, • recourse to pre-trained systems or • tools provided by third parties and • how these have been used, • integrated or • modified by the provider	A: Safety plan B: DoS and AI safety report (Myklebust et al., 2025) C: Tool validation document
(b) The design specifications of the system, namely the general logic of the AI system and of the algorithms; the key design choices including the **rationale and assumptions** made, also with regard to persons or groups of persons on which the system is intended to be used The main classification choices; what the system is designed to optimize for and the relevance of the different parameters The description of the expected output and output quality of the system The decisions about any possible trade-off made regarding the technical solutions adopted to comply with the requirements set out in Title III, Chapter 2	A: Introduction, DoS, and compliance with regulations and standards B: Introduction, DoS and Compliance with Regulations and standards C: User manual

AI Act requirements	Link to A: Safety plan chapters B: Safety case chapters C: Named Safety case references
(c) The description of the system architecture explaining how software components build on or feed into each other and integrate into the overall processing The computational resources used to develop, train, test, and validate the AI system	A: DoS and AI safety report (Myklebust et al., 2025) B: DoS, System architecture description (Myklebust et al., 2018) and AI safety report (Myklebust et al., 2025) C: System architecture description
(d) Where relevant, the data requirements in terms of datasheets describing the training methodologies and techniques and the training datasets used, including a general description of these datasets, information about their provenance, scope, and main characteristics How the data was obtained and selected; labelling procedures (e.g. for supervised learning), data cleaning methodologies (e.g. outliers detection)	A: SW and data, AI B: Data quality and AI Safety report (Myklebust et al., 2025) C: Data safety management plan (SCSC Guide) and relevant documents mentioned in this plan
(e) Assessment of the human oversight measures needed in accordance with Article 14, including an assessment of the technical measures needed to facilitate the interpretation of the outputs of AI systems by the deployers, in accordance with Articles 13(3)(d)	A: Human aspects B: Human aspects and oversight (Myklebust et al., 2025) C: AI Safety report
(f) Where applicable, a detailed description of pre-determined changes to the AI system and its performance, together with all the relevant information related to the technical solutions adopted to ensure continuous compliance of the AI system with the relevant requirements set out in Title III, Chapter 2	A: Compliance with regulations and standards B: Compliance with regulations and standards, AI safety report (Myklebust et al., 2025) C: AI Safety report (Myklebust et al., 2025)
(g) The validation and testing procedures used, including information about the validation and testing data used and their main characteristics; metrics used to measure accuracy, robustness, and compliance with other relevant requirements set out in Title III, Chapter 2, as well as potentially discriminatory impacts Test logs and all test reports dated and signed by the responsible persons, including with regard to predetermined changes as referred to under point (f)	A: Planning the safety activities B: Safety verification and validation, compliance with regulations and standards (Myklebust et al., 2025) C: Test, analyses, and verification and validation reports
(h) Cybersecurity measures put in place	A: Not part of this book B: Should be a separate cybersecurity case (EN TS 50701 and ISO/SAE 21434) C: Cybersecurity case

AI Act requirements	Link to A: Safety plan chapters B: Safety case chapters C: Named Safety case references
3. Detailed information about the monitoring, functioning and control of the AI system, in particular with regard to: Its capabilities and limitations in performance, including the degrees of <u>accuracy</u> for specific persons or groups of persons on which the system is intended to be used and the overall expected level of accuracy in relation to its intended purpose The foreseeable unintended outcomes and sources of risks to health and safety, fundamental rights and discrimination in view of the intended purpose of the AI system The human oversight measures needed in accordance with Article 14, including the technical measures put in place to facilitate the interpretation of the outputs of AI systems by the deployers Specifications on input data, as appropriate	A: Chapters 6 and 16 B: AI safety report (Myklebust et al., 2025) C: User manual
3. A description of the appropriateness of the <u>performance metrics</u> for the specific AI system	A: Chapter 6 B: AI safety report (Myklebust et al., 2025) C: AI System Performance Metrics Report
4. A detailed description of the risk management system in accordance with Article 9	A: Chapters 8 and 12 B: Safety management report and AI Safety report (Myklebust et al., 2025). C: Safety management report
5. A description of relevant changes made by the provider to the system through its lifecycle	A: Chapter 8 B: AI safety report (Myklebust et al., 2025) C: AI safety report and release notes
6. A list of the harmonized standards applied in full or in part, the references of which have been published in the Official Journal of the European Union; where no such harmonized standards have been applied, a detailed description of the solutions adopted to meet the requirements set out in Title III, Chapter 2, including a list of other relevant standards and technical specifications applied	A: Chapter 8 B: Compliance and AI safety report (RAMS 2025) C: Compliance report
7. A copy of the EU declaration of conformity	A: Chapter 8 B: Compliance (Myklebust et al., 2025) C: Declaration of conformity (ISO/IEC 17050 series)
8. A detailed description of the system in place to evaluate the AI system performance in the post-market phase in accordance with Article 61, including the post-market monitoring plan referred to in Article 61(3)	A: Chapters 6 and 10 B: AI and safety lifecycles C: Post-market analysis report

Appendix C: Definitions

ISO 26262-1:2018 3.143 safety plan: A plan to manage and guide the execution of the safety activities of a project, including dates, milestones, tasks, deliverables, responsibilities and resources.

EN 50126-1:2017. 3.73 safety plan: A documented set of time scheduled activities, resources and events serving to implement the organization, responsibilities, procedures, activities, capabilities and resources that together ensure that an item will satisfy given safety requirements relevant to a given contract or project.

The agile safety plan (TASP): The agile safety plan should be like the safety plans as defined above but also be adaptive, flexible, and arrange for effective solutions. The plan shall be presented regularly to the assessor Certification Body

Note 1: The agile safety plan forces the manufacturer to be specific about the safety process, enabling the assessor to be proactive and to plan the work according to the schedule. It is efficient to build the safety plan by inserting information when it becomes available—an agile approach that will also result in increased safety awareness and understanding

ISO 26262-1:2018. 3.185 work product. Documentation resulting from one or more associated requirements of ISO 26262

Note 1 to entry: The documentation can be in the form of a single document containing the complete information for the work product or a set of documents that together contain the complete information for the work product.

Definitions as presented in the AI Act Article 3 (Regulation 2024/1689)

(1) "AI system" means a machine-based system that is designed to operate with varying levels of autonomy and that may exhibit adaptiveness after deployment, and that, for explicit or implicit objectives, infers, from the input it receives, how to generate outputs such as predictions, content, recommendations, or decisions that can influence physical or virtual environments.

(3) "provider" means a natural or legal person, public authority, agency or other body that develops an AI system or a general-purpose AI model or that has an AI system or a general-purpose AI model developed and places it on the market or puts the AI system into service under its own name or trademark, whether for payment or free of charge.

(4) "deployer" means a natural or legal person, public authority, agency or other body using an AI system under its authority except where the AI system is used in the course of a personal non-professional activity.

(14) "safety component" means a component of a product or of an AI system which fulfils a safety function for that product or AI system, or the failure or malfunctioning of which endangers the health and safety of persons or property.

(20) "conformity assessment" means the process of demonstrating whether the requirements set out in Chapter III, Section 2 relating to a high risk AI system have been fulfilled.

(21) "conformity assessment body" means a body that performs third-party conformity assessment activities, including testing, certification and inspection.

(23) "substantial modification" means a change to the AI system after its placing on the market or putting into service which is not foreseen or planned in the initial conformity assessment by the provider and as a result of which the compliance of the AI system with the requirements set out in Title III, Chapter 2 of this Regulation is affected or results in a modification to the intended purpose for which the AI system has been assessed.

BSI PAS 1884:2021 3.1.12 handover process by which the sustained dynamic driving task function transitions either from a human driver to an automated driving system or from an automated driving system to a human driver.

Appendix D: Acronyms (Table D.1)

Table D.1 Acronyms

ADK	Accessory Development Kit	MRC	Minimum Risk Condition
AIS	Automatic Identification System	ODD	Operational Design Domain
API	Application Programming Interface	OEDR	Object and Event Detection and Response
AS	Autonomous Systems	OEM	Original Equipment Manufacturers
CBD	Contract-based design	PAS	Publicly Available Specification
COTS	Commercial Off The Shelf	PL	Programming Language
CSI	Common Safety Indicators	RAG	Retrieval-augmented generation
DDT	Dynamic Driving Task	RAS	Reliability, Availability, and Serviceability
DIA	Development Interface Agreement	RASIC	Responsible, Accountable, Supporting, Informed, Consulted
DL	Description Language	ROC	Remote Operation Centre
DOS	Description of System	SAR	Safety Assessment Report (generic safety)
DCAS	Driver Control Assistance System	SAR	Search and Rescue (maritime terminology)
EEA	European Economic Area	SC	Safety Case
EMC	Electro Magnetic Compatibility	SDK	Standard Development Kit
EU	European Union	SME	Small and Medium Enterprises)
FPGA	Field Programmable Gate Array	SOLAS	Safety of Life at Sea
FSA	Formal Safety Assessment (IMO)	SPI	Safety Performance Indicators
FVL	Full Variable Language	SRAC	Safety Related Application Condition
GSN	Goal Structuring Notation	TSR	Technical Safety Report
HARA	Hazard and Risk Analysis	TTM	Time To Market
HW	Hardware	UPICS	User Programmable Integrated Circuits
IMO	International Maritime Organization		
LLM	Large Language Model		
LVL	Limited Variable Language		
MED	Maritime Equipment Directive		
MLDL	Machine Learning Development Lifecycle		
MLIL	Machine Learning Implementation Lifecycle		

References to Regulations and Directives Mentioned in This Book

The regulations and directives with a bullet point are not mentioned in the AI Act

REG.1 Electromagnetic Compatibility (EMC) Directive 2014/30/EU

REG.2 Radio Equipment Directive (RED) 2014/53/EU

REG.3 Construction Products Regulation (CPR) 305/2011

REG.4 Equipment for potentially explosive atmospheres (ATEX) Directive 2014/34/EU. The ATEX directive is complementary to the AI Act

REG.5 Regulation (EU) 2024/1689 (AI Act)

REG.6 85/374/EEC (Council Directive concerning liability for defective products)

REG.7 Directive 2002/58/EC (Privacy in electronic communications)

REG.8 Commission Recommendation 2003/361 (SME Definition)

REG.9 Regulation (EC) 300/2008 (Aviation security)

REG.10 Regulation (EC) 765/2008 (Accreditation and market surveillance)

REG.11 Decision 768/2008/EC (Framework for product marketing)

REG.12 Regulation (EU) 167/2013 (Agricultural and forestry vehicles)

REG.13 Regulation (EU) 168/2013 (Two- or three-wheel vehicles and quadricycles)

REG.14 Directive 2014/90/EU (Marine equipment)

REG.15 Regulation (EU) 2024/1975 amending the MED in force from 4 September 2024

REG.16 Directive (EU) 2016/797 (Interoperability of the rail system)

REG.17 Regulation (EU) 2016/679 (General Data Protection Regulation, GDPR)

REG.18 Regulation (EU) 2017/745 (Medical devices)

REG.19 Regulation (EU) 2017/746 (In vitro diagnostic medical devices)

REG.20 Regulation (EU) 2018/858 (Motor vehicle approval and market surveillance)

REG.21 Regulation (EU) 2018/1139 (Civil aviation safety)

REG.22 Directive (EU) 2019/882 (Accessibility for products and services)

REG.23 Regulation (EU) 2019/1020 (Market surveillance and compliance of products)

© The Author(s) 2025

T. Myklebust et al., *The AI Act and The Agile Safety Plan*, SpringerBriefs in Computer Science, https://doi.org/10.1007/978-3-031-80504-2

REG.24 Regulation (EU) 2019/2144 (Motor vehicle safety and road user protection)

REG.25 Directive (EU) 2020/1828 (Consumer protection and representative actions)

REG.26 Regulation (EU) 2022/2065 (Digital Services Act)

REG.27 Directive 2022/2557 (Resilience of critical entities)

REG.28 Regulation (EU) 2023/988 (General product safety)

REG.29 REGULATION (EU) 2023/2854 OF THE EUROPEAN PARLIAMENT AND OF THE COUNCIL of 13 December 2023 on harmonised rules on fair access to and use of data and amending Regulation (EU) 2017/2394 and Directive (EU) 2020/1828 (Data Act)

REG.30 UNECE regulation 156:2021 Software update and software update management system

REG.31 COMMISSION IMPLEMENTING REGULATION (EU) 2022/1426 of 5 August 2022 laying down rules for the application of Regulation (EU) 2019/2144 of the European Parliament and of the Council as regards uniform procedures and technical specifications for the type-approval of the automated driving system (ADS) of fully automated vehicles

REG.32 COMMISSION REGULATION (EU) 2016/919 of 27 May 2016 on the technical specification for interoperability relating to the 'control-command and signalling' subsystems of the rail system in the European Union

Reference of the Standards Mentioned in This Book

STD1. BIPM JCGM GUM-6:2020—Guide to the Expression of Uncertainty in Measurement—Part 6: Developing and Using Measurement Models

STD2. BSI PAS 1881:2022—Assuring the operational safety of automated vehicles

STD3. BSI PAS 1882:2021—Data collection and management for automated vehicle trials

STD4. BSI PAS 1883:2020—Operational Design Domain (ODD) taxonomy for an automated driving system (ADS

STD5. BSI PAS 1884:2021 Safety operators in automated vehicle testing and trialling—Guide

STD6. Data Safety Initiative Working Group. (2024). Data safety guidance (Version 3.6). Safety-Critical Systems Club.

STD7. DIN SPEC 92005:2024-03—Artificial Intelligence—Uncertainty Quantification in Machine Learning

STD8. DNV-RP-0671:2023—Assurance of AI-Enabled Systems

STD9. EN 50126-2:2017—Railway Applications—The Specification and Demonstration of Reliability, Availability, Maintainability, and Safety (RAMS)

STD10. EN 50128:2011—Railway Applications—Communication, Signaling, and Processing Systems—Software for Railway Control and Protection Systems

STD11. EN 50129:2018—Railway Applications—Communication, Signaling, and Processing Systems—Safety-Related Electronic Systems for Signaling

STD12. EN 50716:2023—Railway Applications—Requirements for Software Development

STD13. IEC 31010:2019—Risk Management—Risk Assessment Techniques

STD14. IEC 61131-3:2013—Programmable Controllers—Part 3: Programming Languages

STD15. IEC 61508:2010—Functional Safety of Electrical/Electronic/Programmable Electronic Safety-Related Systems

STD16. IEC TS 61508-2-1: Draft 2024. Functional safety of electrical/electronic/programmable electronic safety-related systems Part 2-1: Requirements for complex semiconductors

© The Author(s) 2025

T. Myklebust et al., *The AI Act and The Agile Safety Plan*, SpringerBriefs in Computer Science, https://doi.org/10.1007/978-3-031-80504-2

STD17. IEC TS 61508-6-1: Draft 2024 Treatment of hardware or software developed to iso 26262

STD18. IEC 61784-3:2021—Industrial Communication Networks—Profiles—Part 3: Functional Safety Fieldbuses—General Rules and Profile Definitions

STD19. IEC 62443 Series—Security for Industrial Automation and Control Systems

STD20. IEC 62381:2012—Commissioning of Electrical, Instrumentation, and Control Systems in the Process Industry—Specific Phases

STD21. IEC 62708:2015—Documents Kinds for Electrical and Instrumentation Projects in the Process Industry

STD22. IEEE P2851.1:2023—Standard for Functional Safety Data Format for Interoperability within the Dependability Lifecycle

STD23. ISO 9001:2015—Quality Management Systems

STD24. ISO 24089:2023—Road Vehicles—Software Update Engineering

STD25. ISO 26262-1:2018—Road Vehicles—Functional Safety

STD26. ISO 26262-8:2018—Road Vehicles—Functional Safety—Supporting Processes

STD27. ISO 21448:2022—Safety of the Intended Functionality (SOTIF)

STD28. ISO 31000:2018—Risk Management—Guidelines

STD29. ISO TS 5083: Draft 2024. Road vehicles. Safety for automated driving systems design, verification and validation

STD30. ISO/PAS 8800: 2024-12—Safety and Artificial Intelligence in Road Vehicles

STD31. ISO/IEC 42001:2023—Information Technology—Artificial Intelligence—Management System

STD32. ISO/IEC 5338:2023—Information Technology—Artificial Intelligence—AI System Life Cycle Processes

STD33. ISO/IEC 5469:2024—Artificial Intelligence—Functional Safety and AI Systems

STD34. ISO/IEC TS 22440—Artificial Intelligence—Functional Safety and AI Systems—Requirements

STD35. ISO/IEC 23894:2023—Information Technology—Artificial Intelligence—Guidance on Risk Management

STD36. ISO/IEC 17050-1:2004 Conformity assessment—Supplier's declaration of conformity—Part 1: General requirements

STD37. ISO/IEC 17050-2:2004 Conformity assessment—Supplier's declaration of conformity—Part 2: Supporting documentation

STD38. ISO/IEC/IEEE 24765:2017—Systems and Software Engineering Vocabulary

STD39. ISO 8000-1:2022—Data Quality—Overview

STD40. ISO/SAE 21434:2021—Road Vehicles—Cybersecurity Engineering

STD41. ITU Telecommunication X.1373:2017—Secure Software Update Capability for Intelligent Transportation System Communication Devices

STD42. ETSI GR SAI-007:2023—Explicability and Transparency of AI Processing

STD43. MIL-STD-882E:2012 System safety

STD44. NIST AI 100-1:2023—Framework: Artificial Intelligence Risk Management

STD45. Offshore Norge. (2023). Recommended guidelines for application of IEC 61508 and IEC 61511 in the Norwegian petroleum industry (Rev. 06). Norwegian Oil and Gas Association.

STD46. SAE J3016—Taxonomy and Definitions for Terms Related to Driving Automation Systems for On-Road Motor Vehicles

STD47. SAE AVSC00002202004:2020—AVSC Best Practice for Describing an Operational Design Domain (ODD)

STD48. SAE J3101—Power Requirements for Automotive Computing Platforms

STD49. SCSC Assurance Case Working Group. (2021). GSN Community Standard: Version 3. Safety-Critical Systems Club (SCSC).

STD50. UL 4600:2023—Safety for the Evaluation of Autonomous Products

STD51. UL 5500:2018—Standard for Safety—Remote Software Updates

STD52. CEN/CLC/TR 17894 Artificial Intelligence Conformity. To be published.

STD53. ISO 34501:2022 Road vehicles—Test scenarios for automated driving systems—Vocabulary

STD54. ISO 34502:2022 Road vehicles—Test scenarios for automated driving systems—Scenario based safety evaluation framework

STD55. ISO 34503:2023 Road Vehicles—Test scenarios for automated driving systems—Specification for operational design domain

STD56. ISO 34504:2024 Road vehicles—Test scenarios for automated driving systems—Scenario categorization

STD57. ISO 34505 draft Road vehicles—Test scenarios for automated driving systems—Scenario evaluation and test case generation

STD58. EN 18031 series: EN 18031-1 covering article 3.3 (d) "radio equipment does not harm the network or its functioning nor misuse network resources, thereby causing an unacceptable degradation of service". EN 18031-2 covering article 3.3 (e) "processing data, namely Internet connected radio equipment, childcare radio equipment, toys radio equipment and wearable radio equipment". EN 18031-3 covering article 3.3 (f) "radio equipment processing virtual money or monetary value"

STD59. IEC 61511:2016 series. Functional safety—Safety instrumented systems for the process industry sector

References to Literature

Abushama, H. M., Alassam, H. A., & Elhaj, F. A. (2021, February). The effect of test-driven development and behavior-driven development on project success factors: A systematic literature review based study. In *2020 International Conference on Computer, Control, Electrical, and Electronics Engineering (ICCCEEE)* (pp. 1–9). IEEE.

ACWG. (2021). *Goal structuring notation community standard*. SCSC.

Adadi, A., & Berrada, M. (2018). Peeking inside the black-box: A survey on explainable artificial intelligence (XAI). *IEEE Access, 6*, 52138–52160.

Arrieta, A. B., Díaz-Rodríguez, N., Del Ser, J., Bennetot, A., Tabik, S., Barbado, A., Garcia, S., Gil-Lopez, S., Molina, D., Benjamins, R., Chatila, R., & Herrera, F. (2020). Explainable Artificial Intelligence (XAI): Concepts, taxonomies, opportunities and challenges toward responsible AI. *Information Fusion, 58*, 82–115.

Carter, H. G., Chan, A., Vinegar, C., & Rupert, J. (2023). Concerns with using Python in machine learning flight critical applications. In *Presented at the Vertical Flight Society's 79th Annual Forum & Technology Display, West Palm Beach, FL.*

Cummings, M. L., Wheeler, B., & Kliem, J. A. (2024, July). *Root cause analysis of a self-driving car dragging a pedestrian*. Retrieved from https://www.researchgate.net/profile/Missy-Cummings/publication/382158234_A_Root_Cause_Analysis_of_a_Self-_Driving_Car_Dragging_a_Pedestrian/links/6691c2d63e0edb1e0fe0f818/A-Root-Cause-Analysis-of-a-Self-Driving-Car-Dragging-a-Pedestrian.pdf

Dawson, J., & Garikapati, D. (2021, April). Extending ISO26262 to an operationally complex system. In *2021 IEEE International Systems Conference (SysCon)* (pp. 1–7). IEEE.

Der Kiureghian, A., & Ditlevsen, O. (2009). Aleatory or epistemic? Does it matter? *Structural Safety, 31*(2), 105–112.

DFØ. (2023). *SSA-S (Smidigavtalen)*. Retrieved from https://anskaffelser.no/verktoy/maler/ssa-s-smidigavtalen

DNV. (2023). *RP-0671 assurance of AI-enabled systems*. DNV.

DSIWG. (2024, April 14). *Data safety guidance*. SCSC.

EA. (2022, June 29). *The European Commission published the revised 'Blue Guide' on the implementation of EU product rules 2022*. Retrieved from https://european-accreditation.org/the-european-commission-published-the-revised-blue-guide-on-the-implementation-of-eu-product-rules-2022/

EASA & Daedalean. (2024, January 23). *Concepts of design assurance for neural networks (CoDANN) Part II*. Retrieved from https://www.easa.europa.eu/en/downloads/128161/en

Endsley, M. R. (1995). Measurement of situation awareness in dynamic systems. *Human Factors, 37*(1), 65–84.

© The Author(s) 2025
T. Myklebust et al., *The AI Act and The Agile Safety Plan*, SpringerBriefs in Computer Science, https://doi.org/10.1007/978-3-031-80504-2

European Commission. (2018, December 19). *Guide for the Electromagnetic Compatibility Directive (Directive 2014/30/EU)*. European Commission

EU. (2024a). *European AI office*. Retrieved September 24, 2024, from https://digital-strategy. ec.europa.eu/en/policies/ai-office

EU. (2024b). *Notified bodies*. Retrieved September 24, 2024, from https://single-market-economy. ec.europa.eu/single-market/goods/building-blocks/notified-bodies_en

EU. (2024c). *Harmonised standards*. Retrieved September 24, 2024, from https://single-market-economy.ec.europa.eu/single-market/european-standards/harmonised-standards_en

EU. (2024d). *Technical documentation and EU declaration of conformity*. Retrieved September 24, 2024, from https://europa.eu/youreurope/business/product-requirements/compliance/technical-documentation-conformity/index_en.htm

EU. (2024e). *Conformity assessment*. Retrieved September 24, 2024, from https://single-market-economy.ec.europa.eu/single-market/goods/building-blocks/conformity-assessment_en

EU. (2024f). *Common safety methods (CSMs)*. Retrieved September 24, 2024, from https://www.era.europa.eu/domains/safety-management/common-safety-methods_en

EU. (2024g). *Data Act explained*. Retrieved September 25, 2024, from https://digital-strategy.ec.europa.eu/en/factpages/data-act-explained

EU. (2024h). *Frequently asked questions data act*. Retrieved from https://digital-strategy.ec.europa.eu/en/library/commission-publishes-frequently-asked-questions-about-data-act

FDA. (2002, January 11). *General principles of software validation; Final guidance for industry and FDA staff*. Retrieved from https://www.fda.gov/media/73141/download

Furnham. (2005). *The psychology of behaviour at work*. Psychology Press.

Håbrekke, S., Hauge, S., & Lundteigen, M. A. (2023). *Guideline for follow-up of Safety Instrumented Systems (SIS) in the operating phase*. APOS project report, SINTEF, Report No. 2023:00107. ISBN 978-82-14-07939-5.

Hanssen, G. K., Stålhane, T., & Myklebust, T. (2018). *SafeScrum®-Agile development of safety-critical software*. Springer.

Harney, L., Parsons, M., Hampton, P., Rivett, R., & Owen, W. (2021). *30 years of safer systems: Three decades of work in the field of safety-critical systems as told through the SCSC newsletter*. Independently Published.

Haugen, S., & Rausand, M. (2011). *Risk assessment*. Retrieved from https://www.ntnu.edu/documents/624876/1277591044/chapt04-rac.pdf/3eb85fbd-eadf-4f55-a9b7-d39bcad42d8a

Hawkins, R., Osborne, M., Parsons, M., Nicholson, M., McDermid, J., & Habli, I. (2022). Guidance on the safety assurance of autonomous systems in complex environments (SACE). *arXiv preprint arXiv:2208.00853*.

HMSO. (1992). *HSE: Health and safety executive: The tolerability of risk from nuclear power stations*.

IEEE Standards Committee. (1990). IEEE standard glossary of software engineering terminology. *IEEE Standard, 610*, 12.

IMO. (2018, April 9). *Revised guidelines for formal safety assessment (FSA) for use in the IMO rule-making process*. Retrieved from https://wwwcdn.imo.org/localresources/en/OurWork/HumanElement/Documents/MSC-

Jakimi, A., & Elkoutbi, M. (2009). Automatic code generation FromUML Statechart. *International Journal of Engineering and Technology, 1*(2), 1793–8236.

Khastgir, S., Sivencrona, H., Dhadyalla, G., Billing, P., Birrell, S., & Jennings, P. (2017, October). Introducing ASIL inspired dynamic tactical safety decision framework for automated vehicles. In *2017 IEEE 20th international conference on intelligent transportation systems (ITSC)* (pp. 1–6). IEEE.

Kundu, D., Samanta, D., & Mall, R. (2013). Automatic code generation from unified modelling language sequence diagrams. *IET Software, 7*(1), 12–28.

Lee, J. D., Wickens, C. D., Liu, Y., & Boyle, L. N. (2017). *Designing for people: An introduction to human factors engineering* (3rd ed.). Create Space.

Lenka, R. K., Kumar, S., & Mamgain, S. (2018, October). Behavior driven development: Tools and challenges. In *2018 International Conference on Advances in Computing, Communication Control and Networking (ICACCCN)* (pp. 1032–1037). IEEE.

Meritt, R. (2020, September 3). *What is MLOps?* Retrieved from https://blogs.nvidia.com/blog/what-is-mlops/

Myhre, B., Hellandsvik, A., & Petersen, S. (2019, October). A responsibility-centered approach to defining levels of automation. *Journal of Physics: Conference Series, 1357*(1), 012027.

Myklebust, T., & Okoh, P. (2022). Functional safety. Sprints and Kanban approach in practice. In *ISSC 40 International Conference on System Safety. Cincinnati 2022*.

Myklebust, T., & Stålhane, T. (2018). *The agile safety case*. Springer.

Myklebust, T., & Stålhane, T. (2021). *Functional safety and proof of compliance*. Springer.

Myklebust, T., & Stålhane, T. (2022, June). Purchasers and integrators of safety components and products, which information should they ask for? In *PSAM16, Hawaii*.

Myklebust, T., Stålhane, T., Hanssen, G. K., Wien, T., & Haugset, B. (2014). Scrum, documentation and the IEC 61508-3: 2010 software standard. In *International Conference on Probabilistic Safety Assessment and Management (PSAM)*.

Myklebust, T., Lyngby, N., & Stålhane, T. (2016a). The agile safety plan. In *PSAM13*.

Myklebust, T, Stålhane, T, & Lyngby, N. (2016b). An agile development process for petrochemical safety conformant software. In *RAMS Symposium, Tucson USA*.

Myklebust, T., Stålhane, T., Baines, R., & Hanssen, G. K. (2017). *The agile hazard log approach*. ESREL.

Myklebust, T., Lyngby, N., & Stålhane, T. (2018a). Agile practices when developing safety systems. *PSAM14, Los Angeles*.

Myklebust, T., Hellandsvik, A., Eriksen, J., & Hanssen, G. (2018b). The agile FMEA approach. In *SCSC The 26th Safety-Critical Systems Symposium*.

Myklebust, T., Stålhane, T., & Hanssen, G. K. (2019). *Analysis first development for agile development of safety critical software*. ESREL.

Myklebust, T., Stålhane, T., & Hanssen, G. (2020, August). Agile safety case and DevOps for the automotive industry. In *30th European Safety and Reliability Conference and the 15th Probabilistic Safety Assessment and Management Conference*.

Myklebust, T., Stålhane, T., Jenssen, G. D., & Haug, I. (2021). *TrustMe, we have a safety case for the public*. ESREL.

Myklebust, T., Stålhane, T., & Vatn, D. M. K. (2025, January). Which chapters and topics should be included in a safety case? In *Paper presented at 71st Annual Reliability and Maintainability Symposium (RAMS 2025), Miramar Beach, Florida*.

Okoh, P., & Myklebust, T. (2024a). Mapping to IEC 61508 the hardware safety integrity of elements developed to ISO 26262. In *Safety and reliability* (pp. 1–17). Taylor & Francis.

Okoh, P., & Myklebust, T. (2024b). Mapping to IEC 61508 software developed to ISO 26262. In *Safety and reliability* (pp. 1–16). Taylor & Francis.

Panigutti, C., Hamon, R., Hupont, I., Fernandez Llorca, D., Fano Yela, D., Junklewitz, H., Scalzo, S., Mazzini, G., Sanchez, I., Soler Garrido J., & Gomez, E. (2023, June). The role of explainable AI in the context of the AI act. In *Proceedings of the 2023 ACM conference on fairness, accountability, and transparency* (pp. 1139–1150).

Patkar, N., Chiş, A., Stulova, N., & Nierstrasz, O. (2021, October). Interactive behavior-driven development: a low-code perspective. In *2021 ACM/IEEE International Conference on Model Driven Engineering Languages and Systems Companion (MODELS-C)* (pp. 128–137). IEEE.

PractiTest. (2024). *Test sets & runs*. Retrieved August 08, 2024, from https://www.practitest.com/help/test-planning-and-execution/test-sets-and-runs/#test-set-structure

Redmill, F. (2010). *ALARP explored*. School of Computing Science Technical Report Series.

Risk Engineering. (2024). *Risk acceptability and tolerability*. Retrieved September 24, 2024, from https://risk-engineering.org/risk-acceptability-tolerability/

Rouse, M. (2016, December 5). *Software library*. Retrieved from https://www.techopedia.com/definition/3828/software-library

Sheridan, T. B., Verplank, W. L., & Brooks, T. L. (1978, November). Human/computer control of undersea teleoperators. In *NASA Ames Research Center, The 14th Annual Conference on Manual Control*.

Stålhane, T., & Johnsen, S. O. (2019). *Software errors and human reliability*. ESREL.

Stålhane, T., & Myklebust, T. (2021). Trust case and the link to safety case. In *SAFE 9th International Conference on Safety and Security Engineering, Rome, Italy*

Tank, U. (2023, November 30). *Verification vs validation testing: Key differences*. Retrieved from https://testsigma.com/blog/verification-vs-validation-testing/

van Leeuwen, K. G., Hedderich, D. M., Harvey, H., & Schalekamp, S. (2024). How AI should be used in radiology: Assessing ambiguity and completeness of intended use statements of commercial AI products. *Insights into Imaging, 15*(1), 51.

Vatn, D. M. K., & Mikalef, P. (2024). Theorizing XAI - A layered concept being multidisciplinary at its core. In *Proceedings of the 30th Americas Conference on Information Systems (AMCIS), Salt Lake City*.

Wang, Y., & Wagner, S. (2018). Combining STPA and BDD for safety analysis and verification in agile development: A controlled experiment. In *Agile Processes in Software Engineering and Extreme Programming: 19th International Conference, XP 2018, Porto, Portugal, May 21–25, 2018, Proceedings 19* (pp. 37–53). Springer.

Widen, W. H., & Koopman, P. (2023). The awkward middle for automated vehicles: Liability attribution rules when humans and computers share driving responsibilities. *Jurimetrics Journal, 64*(1), 41–78.

Young, W., & Leveson, N. G. (2014). An integrated approach to safety and security based on systems theory. *Communications of the ACM, 57*(2), 31–35.